Bob Howard
676 N. 30th
C/S, CO 80904

1248

JOSEPH
HOPKINS
TWICHELL

Mark Twain's Friend and Pastor

By LEAH A. STRONG

❀ ❀ ❀ ❀ ❀

UNIVERSITY
of GEORGIA PRESS *Athens*

To My

MOTHER AND FATHER

Contents

Preface

A "COMPANIONSHIP which to me stands first after Livy's"—
in these words Mark Twain described his friendship with the
Reverend Joseph Hopkins Twichell, pastor of the Asylum Hill
Congregational Church in Hartford, Connecticut. Yet, in the
studies of Twain's life and writings, Twichell is mentioned briefly,
if at all, and with very few facts of his life given. He has been
condemned by some for suppressing Clemens' spontaneity by his
own stodgy Puritanism; he has been likewise condemned by others for not making Twain a professing Christian. He has been
described in various places as tall, short, slender, rotund, friendly,
and austere. Even his name has been spelled *Twitchell* as well as
Twichell. According to the familiar Twain sources, he did his
graduate divinity work at Yale, or perhaps Union. He was a chaplain in the Civil War for three, or sometimes four, years. The
contradictions in factual details are not particularly important;
his effect on the man Samuel Clemens and the writer Mark Twain
is important, however, for no one seems to doubt that their relationship was as close as any friendship which Twain had in his
adult years.

The idea for this present study developed over a period of
years as the writer became more and more aware of the frequency
of Twichell references in Twain materials, and the contradictions
that existed. What started as an analysis of Twichell's influence
on Twain inevitably developed into a biography as it seemed
more and more obvious that the clues to the existing problems
lay, to a great extent, in the personality and character of Twichell
himself. Surface conclusions left gaps in understanding. Why
should Twain have had for his closest friend a man from a small
Connecticut town, a minister of a wealthy church in the Puritan
tradition? Who was this man Twichell? What kind of person
was he?

It is the object of this study to investigate the life of Twichell, particularly his relationship with Mark Twain. (His own writing, in spite of its volume, does not make him a figure of even minor literary significance.) The first sections deal chronologically with his early years: boyhood, college and divinity studies, and Civil War chaplaincy. The Mark Twain material is divided into four parts. In the first an attempt is made to analyze the beginnings of the friendship on the basis of the personalities and past experiences of both men. The second section deals with what they did together—the extent of their joint activities as individuals, with their families, and in the community. The third concerns religion—Twain's participation in the affairs of Twichell's church. It is not true that their friendship was a thing apart from Twichell's professional life; nor is it true that beyond a certain date they never discussed the personal side of religion, as has been claimed. In the last section the important matter of literary influence is considered. In what ways and to what extent did Twichell influence Twain's writing? Was this influence good or bad for Twain's literary production?

Of greatest value among manuscript sources was *Parish Memorabilia of the Asylum Hill Congregational Church, 1865-1918*, a fourteen-volume set of scrapbooks in the Connecticut State Library in Hartford. These scrapbooks were kept by Twichell during his long pastorate at Asylum Hill. In them he put newspaper clippings, letters, programs, post cards, and many miscellaneous items, all relative to the church, its pastor, members, and friends. Since many of these people were well-known literary, political, and business figures, these scrapbooks are a mine of information of various kinds. Mark Twain items appear frequently. The accuracy of information found in the scrapbooks is of great value. Whenever a mistake occurred in a newspaper, magazine, or other clipping, Twichell made the necessary correction in the margin. He was extremely careful about these corrections, even making the same one repeatedly. When called "Doctor," as he often was, he crossed it out and wrote, "Mister," which he preferred. Referred to as chaplain of a Connecticut regiment during the Civil War, he changed it every time to "71st New York." Sometimes he put comments in the margins, interesting revelations of his character, particularly his wit. Beside one somewhat "flowery" statement, he wrote, "Oh, they had reporters in the old days!" The nature of this collection can be seen in a letter which Twichell attached to the inside cover of Volume I:

Somewhere about 1880 in clearing up my study, I found stored away in pigeon holes &c a considerable quantity of newspaper clippings, and other printed matter, which, being of the nature of parish memorabilia, I felt it a pity to destroy.

I then concieved [*sic*] the idea (wondering that it had never occurred to me before) of a Parish Scrap Book in which such things as composed this accumulation should be placed in order, and preserved, with further like material as it came.

My principal thought was that a collection of the sort illustrating the history of the parish in my time, would be of interest, and perhaps of use, to those coming after me. The project, when once I had entertained it, I liked so well, that I announced it to the people, asking for contributions of memorabilia which they might have saved to add to my stock; by which means it was not a little increased. While, as a rule, I have confined the record to our own separate affairs, I have, in a few instances included relics of occurrences in which we were concerned as incorporate with the general religious community. The *dates* supplied are usually those of the events mentioned under them.

As from year to year the Scrap Book has grown. I have been rather uncomfortably conscious that the pastor figures in it far more largely than his weight and significance as a factor of the parish life would justify. That, however, could scarcely be otherwise.

March. 1892.   Joseph H. Twichell

The chief weakness as research material in the Scrapbooks is in the incompleteness of many items. There are title pages torn from pamphlets which Twichell wrote, complete copies of which seem at present unavailable. The events are often dated, but not the clippings in which the events are related. There is often no identification of newspaper or pamphlet titles. Many of the items are from the *Hartford Courant,* of which Twichell's friend and parishioner, Charles Dudley Warner, was the editor. Some I have succeeded in locating in the *Courant* files at the newspaper offices, but since many of the clippings are from papers in Boston, Springfield, New York, and other places across the country, they were impossible for me to locate. Pamphlets proved particularly difficult, even when the titles were available. Since Twichell corrected any inaccuracies in them, they are reliable sources, though often unidentifiable.

I am indebted to many people who helped in different ways. The Reverend Joseph Hooker Twichell of Washington, Connecticut, told me several anecdotes about his father and directed me to other sources of information of which I might otherwise have been unaware.

Father Walter J. Meagher, professor at Holy Cross College, Worcester, Massachusetts, found for me several items concerning Twichell's friend, Father Joseph B. O'Hagan, chaplain with him during the Civil War and later president of Holy Cross College. This friendship was extremely important in the broadening of Twichell's outlook before his meeting with Twain. Father Meagher made available from the Holy Cross Archives and Library many items which made my study of Father O'Hagan more complete.

The Reverend Fletcher D. Parker, late minister of Immanuel Congregational Church in Hartford, Connecticut, and a long-time student of the writings of Horace Bushnell, read the sections of this work dealing with Bushnell. His church is the descendant (after a merger) of Bushnell's church, and his interest in and knowledge of Bushnell were of great value.

My father, the late Robert L. Strong of Windsor, Connecticut, and my mother, Mrs. Dorothy K. Strong, now of Macon, Georgia, helped in many ways. Their encouragement, assistance, and understanding were never-ending.

I am especially indebted to Dr. Edwin Harrison Cady of Indiana University and Dr. Edd Winfield Parks of the University of Georgia, who both read the entire manuscript and made valuable suggestions.

Many others, too numerous to name, helped at various stages of the work. I am particularly grateful to two friends, Mrs. Hilah F. Newton and Miss Dorothy A. Gentzler of Syracuse, New York, whose enthusiasm and confidence often kept me going.

To all these people who assisted, my thanks.

LEAH A. STRONG

Wesleyan College
Macon, Georgia

I

※

Boyhood

THE LITTLE BOY went running down the dusty, country road, his yellow-backed Shorter Catechism under his arm.[1] Tall for his eight years, wiry and active, he ran past the well-kept houses and through a field where he and his friends had worn a path by using frequently this favorite short-cut. This time he did not look around to see if he were being observed by the owner.

It was spring, and birds and trees seemed much more interesting than school. He wished he could wear his old clothes and ramble through the quiet New England countryside finding his favorite hide-aways. The winter months had been long and cold, and there had been little opportunity for a boy to use up his abundant supply of energy.

He could not be late, or the teacher would be angry. There was a new teacher, too, who expected boys to be on time at the little district school house at Southington Corners, Connecticut. He realized regretfully that he would not have had to run if he had not stopped to look at a bird in a tree and to throw a few stones at a big elm tree that made a wonderful target.

And then it happened—a large smudge on a page of the little book. His father had told him to go straight to school without playing on the way, but he had disobeyed and now there was dirt on his hand and, more important, on the book. He started to cry, but he did not know why. He had soiled other books—and other things, too—but this was not the same. He did not stop to worry about covering with dirt the information about Decrees or Effectual Calling—those things he did not understand completely, anyway, though he could say them.

What are the decrees of God?

The decrees of God are his eternal purpose, according to the

1

Counsel of his own will, whereby for his own glory he hath fore-ordained whatsoever comes to pass.

What is effectual calling?

Effectual calling is a work of God's spirit, where by convincing us of our sin and misery, enlightening our minds in the knowledge of Christ, and renewing our wills, he doth persuade us and enable us to embrace Jesus Christ, freely offered to us in the Gospel.[2]

Arriving just on time, he slipped into his seat. His benchmate looked at him with surprise, for this was an unusual thing—the best ball player in the grade crying?

"What's the matter, Joe?" he whispered.

Joe shoved the little book, with its dirty smudge, into his friend's hand. His friend looked worried, but he still did not understand what there was to cry about. If Joe was upset, however, he would try to help. He took his not-too-clean handkerchief from his pocket, carefully spit on it, wiped the page of the book, and then rubbed it on his knee. After that he blew on it, and with a hesitant smile, handed it back to Joe. It would certainly be clean when it dried.

It was not. The old familiar doctrines were obscured. And even though he did not understand them very well, the little boy was unduly upset. The meaning of the old words did not disturb him. Since everyone he knew well said them, they must be true. His father's hired hand, Pat, did not say them, but he was a Catholic. Sometimes Joe wondered, though. If *fore-ordained* meant *caused to happen,* and if God caused things to happen, then why . . .? It certainly was not God who put the smudge on the page of the book. Thoughts like these were only shadows at this time, although occasionally on a hot summer day he and his friends would lie on the grass, with no adults listening, and try to comprehend these statements for themselves, reluctant to let their parents know that they had questions.

He cried again on his way home that day, and he never knew why. It was too bad. Perhaps he could repair the book later, or maybe he could have a new one.

The boy whose early contact with old doctrines was thus sometimes unhappy was Joseph Hopkins Twichell, later to become Civil War chaplain, minister of a large church in Hartford, Connecticut, for almost fifty years; author, critic, public figure, friend of many literary, religious, civic, and business leaders; and friend and long-time companion of Mark Twain. He was to be the parson in Charles Dudley Warner's *Backlog Studies,* and "Mr. Harris" in Twain's *A Tramp Abroad.* He was to lecture in Hartford, Boston, New York, Chicago, and many other cities; at Yale, Cornell, and other universities. But in the 1840's he was a small boy growing up in a small town in mid-nineteenth century Connecticut.

For a long lifetime he would be a prominent citizen of this state which he was just beginning to know. Connecticut saw many developments in the first sixty years of the nineteenth century. Slowly it changed from an agricultural area to an industrialized section of the country. The early struggles of the settlers with the rocky soil, followed by two wars, the Revolution and the War of 1812, had delayed progress. When the settlement was nearly two centuries old, however, change began in earnest. Industrialization moved rapidly ahead. By 1849 there were 50,700 wage earners manufacturing goods worth over $47,000,000 per year. There were cotton and woolen mills, forges, brass foundries, tanneries, distilleries, ropewalks, gunpowder mills, and carriage manufacturers.

Many of the little industries which would be large companies by the time Joseph was an adult had their beginnings during these years. Eli Terry, for example, took out his first clock patent in 1797; the manufacture of pins in Derby began in 1835. After 1815, single tinware shops were sending out twenty or thirty wagons, and Yankee peddlers made their way across the country. Charles Goodyear, born in New Haven in 1800, obtained his first patent for his vulcanizing process in 1844.

Even before this, in 1842, a manufactory of rubber shoes was opened in New Haven. The Haywood Rubber Company was organized in Colchester in 1847. In 1835-1836, Samuel Colt perfected his patents both in England and America for a pistol with a rotary cylinder with several chambers, to discharge through a single barrel. The efficiency of this weapon was demonstrated in the Mexican and Seminole wars, and in 1848 a plant for its manufacture was established in Hartford. In 1858, 60,000 revolvers were made there; and between 1861 and 1864 Twichell would see many of them in use in the Civil War before he moved to Hartford. Two years before he was born, Frank and Ralph Cheney began to manufacture silk thread from imported raw materials. These are only a few of the infant industries which were making their start in the first half of the century. Many others were also being established—particularly smaller ones to supply the larger companies with parts and materials.[3]

By the time of the Civil War, farming and manufacturing had become about equally important in the state, with approximately the same amount of capital invested in each, and the same number of people engaged in each. An important crop, then as now, was tobacco. Although Twichell would not become much aware of it until he moved to the center of the Connecticut River Valley, as early as 1765 tobacco was exported from Suffield to England. In 1833 the most important discovery was made about the Valley tobacco: that it possessed the firm texture, strong tissue, and smooth surface necessary for cigar wrappers. Raising tobacco soon became one of the most profitable businesses in the state.[4]

While these larger changes were taking place throughout the state in the first half of the century, their effects would not be felt fully until much later. In the meantime, life in the small towns remained much the same as it had been for many years. Small industries might open, perhaps a carriage hardware company to supply nearby manufacturers; farmers might gradually change their crops as word reached them of more profitable things to grow commercially. In village life, however, there was little change in the familiar patterns of life.

In most of the towns, including Southington where boys like Twichell were concerned with problems of school and home, the chief figure in the community was the minister. Although the cities had seen the arrival and acceptance of other denominations, the small town usually had only one major church. Other denominations might be represented by small groups, but the larger congregations remained Congregational. Even the Unitarian Church, which had grown rapidly in Massachusetts, was not present in many Connecticut towns. Thus the Congregational minister was still in most cases the best educated member of the community. After earlier periods of enthusiasm, controversy, and excitement about religion—Jonathan Edwards' "Sinners in the Hands of an Angry God" had been preached in Enfield, Connecticut—the churches in the small towns had continued placidly. In the Brahmin tradition, the minister held the respect of all. He preached; if possible, he wrote; he helped to educate the children. When small-town businessmen and farmers found themselves financially able to send a son to college, it was to prepare that son for the ministry.

Joseph Hopkins Twichell was born in Southington, Connecticut, on May 27, 1838, the son of Deacon Edward Twichell and his first wife, Selina D. Carter. The founder of the family in America had been Joseph Twichell, who was made a freeman of the Massachusetts colony in 1634 and later went to Hartford with Thomas Hooker's group of settlers.

Edward Twichell was born in Wolcott, Connecticut, on September 5, 1810. According to folk tradition, when a young man left Wolcott his future depended on which side of Wolcott Hill he went down. Would his major concern be intellectual or industrial? One route, that taken by Bronson Alcott, led him to Boston, Concord, and Transcendentalism. The other side of the hill led to Waterbury, and Connecticut industry; this had been the route taken by Seth Thomas, the clock manufacturer. Edward Twichell went down the "industrial" side of the hill when he moved to the part of Southington now known as Plantsville. He began his industrial career by learning the tanner's and currier's trade. He soon went into partnership with his teacher, Timothy Higgins, and, as the business prospered, they branched out into making leather belting. In 1850 Twichell became interested in the manufacture of carriage hardware and decided to go into partnership with another local man, Henry D. Smith. He continued this activity until his death in 1863.[5]

Edward seems to have been a reasonably prosperous small-town independent business man. There is no indication of either affluence or poverty in the family affairs. Like many of his contemporaries, he was a God-fearing man with much practical Yankee business sense, who felt that his moderate success was due to his own efforts under Providence. The "efforts" were necessary, but, as he often told his children, so was Providence. Thus he was very active in the affairs of the Southington Congregational Church, which he had joined on April 6, 1834. On September 11, 1851, he was elected deacon, getting 46 of the 50 votes cast.

Universally liked and respected by his business acquaintances and church brethren, Edward provided a comfortable and sensible living for his children. Their childhood was by no means glamorous, except as nineteenth century boys and girls found exciting the pleasures of life in a small Connecticut town. For the young Twichells there was school at the Corners, with delightful walks to and from that school; there was church, perhaps with monotonously long sermons on Sundays, but also with frequent "socials," which the children always enjoyed.

Southington was small and far enough from the Connecticut cities so that to a small boy it seemed to be the whole world. New Haven, Bridgeport, Hartford—Joseph knew people who had been to those places, but for now they were only names to him. That he would not only know all of them, but also be a well-known figure in them was not even in his imagining. For awhile there was Southington, with its fields, meadows, and rolling hills. Boys fished, hiked, played ball, and dreamed.

The Deacon was a good father, strict but kind. Carefully he taught his fast-growing family his own combination of Yankee religion and practicality. Joseph was the oldest; then came Edward, born in 1839; Upson, born in 1843 (died in 1844); and Sarah, born in 1844. In April, 1849, Selina Twichell died, and during the following year Edward married Jane Walkley. The family continued to grow: Mary, born in 1851; Olive, born in 1854; Timothy in 1856; Julia in 1859; and Anna, born in 1862.

The death of his mother was undoubtedly a blow to the ten-year-old boy. It was a confusing time, with a neighbor coming and taking his little sister with her for awhile, leaving Joseph and his brother Edward alone with their silent father. This unhappy and confusing time passed, and the arrival of a step-mother into the family circle was welcomed. She soon became another mother to the growing boy. Later, when he was a chaplain in the Civil War, she kept all the letters he wrote to the family, treasuring them as if she were his real mother.

Although not a college graduate himself, Edward was anxious that his oldest son go to college. First, however, came attendance at the district schoolhouse at the Corners, where Joseph learned his three R's. After that, he attended the Sally Lewis Academy for college preparatory study. Like many similar institutions, the Lewis Academy had a series of teachers who stayed for relatively short periods. The first under whom Joe studied was Stephen Fenn, a pleasant young man who had graduated from Yale in 1849, and taught at the Lewis Academy for only one year before returning to Yale for divinity studies. Young and inexperienced, Mr. Fenn was only moderately successful with his students.

Fenn was followed by the Rev. Mr. Guy B. Day, who remained at the Academy for three years, 1851-1854. His term at the school was beneficial to Joseph and the other students, because Mr. Day, a man really interested in teaching and in education, was not just filling in time between undergraduate work and the ministry. He, too, had been ordained; but he spent his life in educational work, going from Southington to a school in Bridgeport.

The last teacher under whom Joseph studied at Lewis was the Rev. Mr. E. I. Avery, who became Principal in the fall of 1854, and stayed for three and a half years.[6]

At the Lewis Academy the boys were taught according to the best methods of instruction of the time. The worth of intellectual and cultural achievement, the ambition for success, the desire to devote one's life to the service of God and man—these three goals were always present in the day-to-day and long-term life of the school. Intellectuality, personal success, and service did not seem to be contradictory aims to the Yankee mind.

During these years Joseph was also learning from the church. His great dismay over the soiled catechism seems to be the only recorded experience of his childhood which might be considered unusual for a boy growing up in his environment. The pastor of the Southington Congregational Church was the Rev. Mr. Elisha Cowles Jones, who spent thirty-five years in this Southington pastorate. Solid in his theology as well as in his understanding of human nature, Mr. Jones was a quiet man whose influence on the community was steady and good, although he was not a particularly inspired preacher. As he droned through a long sermon, the boys sat in the gallery, sleeping and perspiring on warm Sundays. But Mr. Jones himself *was* an influence on those sleepy boys. When they began to think about their own careers, many of them decided to be like Mr. Jones, to enter the ministry, and to hold a place like his in the estimation of the community. As a result, an unusually large percentage of Southington's young men became ministers.[7]

Of great value to the boy was the one time when he heard the inspired Horace Bushnell preach. It was during a period when Bushnell's name was just beginning to be known throughout the state, a time when his deviations from the norm of nineteenth century Congregationalism were causing excited talk even in the small communities like Southington. Again the words, like many of those in the catechism, were beyond a boy's understanding. The adults talked about Christian nurture, atonement, and the Trinity, some of them becoming very much excited and even talking of heresy. Joseph's father, Deacon Edward Twichell, never said "heresy," however, because many of the ideas of this man Bushnell sounded sensible to him. An unemotional, cautious thinker, he wanted to consider these matters very carefully before he decided on their validity.

He waited for a chance to hear Bushnell preach. He wanted
to see him, to hear him talk, to watch his face—a lot, he felt,
could be discovered about a man that way—and then he would
decide for himself whether or not these ideas should be labeled
"heresy." In the meantime, he said little when others were discussing Bushnell, and his son, realizing his father's interest in
religion, wondered what it was all about.

Eventually the time came when Dr. Bushnell was to preach in
nearby Plainville. Deacon Edward, however, never missed services
at his own church. The story had gotten around that one Sunday,
he and Mr. Jones were the only ones to get through a blizzard
to the little meeting-house. As Mr. Jones looked at his congregation of one, it was reported that he began, "Brethren . . . ah . . .
Deacon Twichell," and then went on with his ninety minute
sermon.

Bushnell's preaching in Plainville was an important occasion.
The Deacon wanted to hear him, and he knew that he would
not be able to go to Bushnell's church in Hartford on a Sunday
morning. He talked it over with his wife, and she, knowing how
important it was to him, agreed that he should go, although she
would not be able to accompany him because of the younger
children in the family. Young Joseph listened to the plans being
made. Just imagine, his father would hear this great man about
whom everyone was talking, this man who had preached in places
much larger than he had ever seen. He wondered what he would
say; it would surely be different from a sermon of Mr. Jones'. He
wondered how he would look, for he must be different from
other men.[8]

On Saturday night, all Deacon Edward said was, "Joseph, if
you want to go to Plainville with me tomorrow, you will have to
get up early and get your chores done. I'm going to be on time,
and I won't wait for you."

When the Deacon got up the next morning, he found his son
sitting quietly in the kitchen, the chores all done, the boy looking
very serious, but excited, already dressed in his "Sunday" suit.

In later years Twichell remembered very little about the sermon itself, except that it was one of the Christian Nurture series.
Although not a large man, Dr. Bushnell appeared impressive
with inspired sincerity sounding in every word. The boy was too
young to understand the complexities of these doctrinal matters,
but he was just the right age for hero-worship. If it would be a
fine thing to be a preacher like Mr. Jones, what would it be to

be like Dr. Bushnell? Even though not understanding all that was said, Joe had not been sleepy. He was impressed by the dynamic power of the man and by the large group of people attending the service, many of whom had traveled a good distance just to go to church.

As father and son rode back to Southington, the father holding the horse's reins loosely, the son sitting very straight beside him, Deacon Edward said over and over, "That was great preaching! Great preaching!" Joseph thought so, too.[9]

One other childhood experience proved to be more important in Joe's adult life than anyone would have realized at the time. An employee of Deacon Twichell's was an Irish boy who lived in the household with the family, a custom then prevalent in New England. Cheerful, often joking and laughing, passionately fond of Ireland, he loved to talk to Joseph, the little fellow who seemed to be interested in so many things. Eventually Joseph would learn Latin and Greek, but his first experience with words strange to his Yankee tongue were those taught him by his Irish companion, and he soon knew the meaning of "mavourneen" and "Erin Go Bragh," and many others. He also learned what he later called "the pathetic Iliad of Ireland's sorrows."[10]

As Twichell himself put it, he was brought up "in a family and community in which religion and philanthropy were principal subjects of interest."[11] The family, the teachers at the Sally Lewis Academy, the Rev. Mr. Elisha Cowles Jones, and Dr. Horace Bushnell—these were the most important formative influences. Southington would hold him for only a short time; when he left for college, he really left permanently. There was little to draw him back, and he had the world to see. Speaker, preacher, friend of *literati,* world traveler, author—these were the things ahead of him.

In 1855 the boy was ready to enter college. Joe, his father, and Mr. Jones had discussed his plans for further education many times. There were three colleges in Connecticut at that time. Besides Yale, there were Trinity College in Hartford (an Episcopalian institution which had received the right of establishment by the state constitution of 1818) and Wesleyan University in Middletown (a Methodist college founded in 1831). The teachers in the Southington schools had almost all been Yale graduates, and they had inspired many of their students with Yale spirit. The location of Southington, twenty-two miles from New Haven, along with the family's Congregationalism, made the decision easy. By now the boy was tall, slender, friendly, but quiet to the point of apparent shyness, serious, religious, and a good athlete. He had gotten what his small town could give him. Some of its influence would make for his later strength. Some of its influence he had to lose before he could become more liberal in attitudes, interests, and points of view.

The things ahead of him were not suspected by the townspeople. He was merely the Deacon's eldest son going off to college.

Just before he left, he saw the local physician and long-time friend of the family, Dr. Barnes. When Joe told the doctor that he was soon to leave for Yale, the doctor told him that he was too young.

"But, Dr. Barnes," said Joseph, "I shall be as old as Frank Jones was when he went."

"Frank Jones! Frank Jones!" he exclaimed. "That's another matter. *He* had *character!*"[12]

II

Yale and Union

IN 1855, in spite of Dr. Barnes' joking opinion, Twichell entered Yale, having proved satisfactorily to the entrance examiners that he was prepared—with a knowledge of Cicero's *Select Orations; The Bucolics, Georgics,* and the first six books of the *Aeneid* of Virgil; Sallust, Andrews and Stoddard's *Latin Grammar;* Jacobs' *Greek Reader;* Xenophon's *Anabasis,* first three books; Professor Sophocles' *Greek Grammar;* Thorman's *Higher Arithmetic,* and Day's *Algebra,* to quadratic equations.[1]

The following four years were important ones, because they were his first break from the quiet town of Southington, still deep in the Brahmin tradition, and still primarily rural. New Haven was fast becoming an industrial center in Connecticut. Yale students could not help but feel a faster pace of life than many of them had known before.

The freshman class in 1855 had 154 members, including many who were to become life-long friends of Twichell. Especially close to him were Edward Carrington, Thomas R. Lounsbury, Robert Stiles, Diodate (Date) Hannahs, and Eugene Smith.

For four years, paying $39 for tuition the first year and $45 per year thereafter, Twichell continued his classical studies. The course of study allowed very little free choice. The first two years consisted of continuing studies in Greek, Latin, Mathematics, and Rhetoric.[2] In the third year those studies were continued, with Natural Philosophy and Astronomy added. During the third term of the junior year there was one elective course, a choice of Modern Languages, Ancient Languages, or Mineralogy.[3] Since Yale University records contain only his semester averages without a list of the individual courses taken, there is no way of knowing which course he elected. His earlier training and later interests would suggest that his choice was probably

11

Ancient Languages. The fourth year curriculum included Astronomy, Mineralogy, and Geology, Moral Philosophy, Political Philosophy, Anatomy, and Theology.[4]

Throughout these four years Joseph studied enough to get by, but did not do any particularly outstanding work. Scholarship was marked on a scale of 4, which represented perfection, with 2 the lowest passing grade. No semester grade above 2.82 is recorded for Twichell, and that height he attained only once, in the second term of his sophomore year. The only grade below the necessary 2 is a 1.56 on the biennial examination of 1859.

His average for the four years was 2.48, placing him eightieth in a graduating class of 105. Most of his close friends did better: Edward Carrington, 3.28; Thomas Lounsbury, 3.08; Eugene Smith, 3.54.

During his junior year one incident occurred which overshadowed all others in its significance to him then and later. Most Yale students at that time belonged to "eating clubs," which made arrangements with local restaurants to serve them as a group for set fees. Twichell and his closest friends belonged to the Crocodile Club, which had its headquarters at the corner of High and Elm Streets. In Yale's history there had been several "town and gown" clashes in New Haven, but for four years all had been peaceful. Yale administrative officers and New Haven authorities, of course, hoped that there would be no serious disturbances.

Gradually, however, very serious trouble was brewing. It started, innocently enough, because the Crocodiles liked to sing on their way to and from their restaurant. When they discovered that their choice of songs was annoying the firemen whose station they passed, their undergraduate, boyish enthusiasm overcame their gentlemanly common sense, and they tried to choose songs which would be sure to annoy the firemen. Day after day, on their way to and from meals, they sang loudly their carefully-selected songs.

On Saturday, February 6, 1858, the firemen retaliated by swaggering around the college yards and buildings, threatening dire reprisals if the students did not stay away from their departmental headquarters. Stone-throwing students, they insisted, had broken windows at the Engine House. They promised to see that no windows were left unshattered on the entire Yale campus if the students disturbed them again.

The undaunted undergraduates sang even more enthusiastically during the next two days. On Monday, February 8, water was "accidentally" thrown on the boisterous singers as they passed the headquarters of the Fire Department's Engine Number 2, on High Street, in the rear of Alumni Hall.

On what was to become, unfortunately, a fatal evening, Tuesday, February 9, 1858, the Crocodiles had successfully passed the Fire House with only an interchange of insults from both sides. Some of the students then decided to go back and settle the matter once and for all. The basic question of the moment involved the crucial point as to whether or not the students had the "right" to sing their songs on the side of the street opposite the Fire House. After much loud arguing, the firemen finally gave in on that one point and were forced to agree that the students did have such a "right."

When another incident of a long struggle seemed to be ending peacefully, and some of the students were leaving, half a dozen firemen from the York Street Company arrived as reinforcements for their besieged brothers of Engine Number 2. Shouting "Now we have them, boys!" the leader of the firemen struck one of the students with a speaking trumpet, a relatively heavy piece of equipment normally used during the noise and confusion of fire-fighting so that directions could be heard.

The departing students returned, and a general brawl ensued. Most of the students carried the then stylish canes or bangers; several of the firemen had hose wrenches. Blows were aimed in all directions; bricks were thrown, and one or two students were badly hurt. Losing to more powerful forces, the Yale men began again to leave.

Suddenly a cry of "Shoot! Shoot!" came from the students. Several shots rang out, and the students quickly scattered.

One fireman was found to be shot through the body. He had been one of the leaders in the fight and had been noticed, just before the shooting, aiming a blow at a prostrate student. He died the following afternoon, leaving a wife and two children.

Many of the circumstances were strange and confusing. Most of the Crocodiles did not know, apparently, that one of their members owned and was carrying a gun. Because of the wide area of the brawl and because some of the students had already turned to leave, many of them honestly did not know who had shouted "Shoot!" nor who had fired the shot.

Yale authorities were extremely anxious to cooperate with New Haven investigators. Town and gown relationships had never been so badly strained before. It was an incident that was hard

to believe—and yet it had most certainly happened. The Crocodiles were all young men from respectable families and were all
satisfactory (and better) students. There was no easy way to
pinpoint the blame. Questioning of the participants by local
police and Yale authorities brought no answers that in any way
clarified the situation.

When the coroner's jury heard the evidence, the matter was
further obscured by the Crocodiles themselves. Those who had
been on the scene and those who had been walking away all
refused to testify. In what has since been a much-used formula
in twentieth century investigations, these mid-nineteenth century
students made use of the Fifth Amendment to the Constitution
and would not say anything that might subject themselves to a
criminal prosecution. In a test case, such right to refuse was
sustained.

Yale authorities were not satisfied with the legal conclusion of
the episode, however, and continued their own investigation,
which resulted in the rustication (suspension) of three Crocodiles: Edward Carrington, Eugene Smith, and Joseph Twichell.
While three young men tried with little success to explain their
suspension to their families and friends at home without revealing any more facts than they had in New Haven, the remaining Crocodiles were questioned again and again.

Convinced of the guilt of one of the three, Yale authorities
were unable to determine the identity of the one who had fired
the shot. Since two innocent men could not justifiably be punished
for a crime committed by another, Yale was forced to allow all
three to return to college.[5]

The whole incident made a tremendous impression on the
young man from Southington whose life had been unstained
previously. Yale tradition is that this incident was the turning
point of Twichell's life: that it was at this time that the previously gay young man became serious and decided to enter the
ministry as some kind of atonement for his part in the affair,
whether or not he had been the one with the gun. While there
is no doubt that he was deeply shaken by it and its effects on his
friends and family at home, there is no reason to believe that it
actually changed the course of his life. He seems to have planned
to enter the ministry long before the incident occurred.

In his adult years Twichell was occasionally asked about the
shooting. His usual reply was of the "no comment" variety. No
matter how he was pressed by a scandal-seeking reporter, he

would say nothing. Finally, in an interview in 1914, fifty-six years after the incident, he broke his silence only to this extent:

> The incident happened truly enough, but I don't know that it had any special bearing on my future. I had intended to go into the ministry. . . .
>
> Yes, I was there, and the fireman died. I didn't fire the shot. That's a long time ago. The poor fellow who fired the shot is dead. I've never talked about it. It wasn't a thing to talk about. . . .[6]

While the name of the person who fired the shot has never been established by Yale or legal authorities, it was generally known that some of the students involved did know the guilty individual's identity, but would not reveal it.

Another fact which entered Yale legend mysteriously was that the guilty Crocodile was graduated in 1859, joined the Union Army in 1861, was killed in battle on March 6, 1865.[7]

One of the casualties in the Battle of St. Mark's River, Florida, on March 6, 1865, was Edward Carrington, Twichell's friend and one of the original three who were suspected.

Much of what happened, and why, remains shrouded. That Twichell did not fire the shot seems clear. That he knew who did seems also sure. That he sympathized rather than condemned is evidenced by his loyalty to Carrington at the time, even when his college education and career were at stake, and by his refusal to identify the man at any time later on. His first son was Edward Carrington Twichell.

Reaction to the episode died slowly in New Haven. College sentiment favored the fireman at first and regretted the shooting as unnecessary. Because no action was taken by the courts, the firemen some months later published a series of so-called "scurrilous Resolutions" about the affair, which transferred college sympathies back to the students. Finally, Yale, finding it advisable to do everything possible to prevent further town and gown disturbances, disbanded the Crocodiles and purchased the Engine House as a storehouse for the college carpenter.

At Yale Twichell's academic honors were few, but significant in view of the kind of minister he was to become in later years. He won two prizes in English composition and a second prize in declamation in his sophomore year, and took a Townsend Premium award for English composition in his senior year.

It is typical of the man that, in spite of these academic honors, he himself mentioned more frequently in later years the fact that he had been stroke on the Yale crew which defeated Harvard in 1859!

After being graduated from Yale in 1859, Twichell was ready to enter divinity school. During his years at Yale, the family finances had improved moderately, his father's business proving to be more profitable than it had been earlier. His first thought was to remain in New Haven to attend the Yale Divinity School. In 1858-1859, however, while he was making up his mind, he could not help but see that Yale's divinity school was somewhat weak. There were two reasons for this decline in an institution which had flourished in earlier years. For one thing, for many years its reputation had depended particularly on the fame of Dr. Nathaniel W. Taylor, Professor of Doctrinal Theology. He was an inspiring teacher and a leader in a movement which had revolted against the narrower orthodoxy of the time. Taylor, however, died in the spring of 1858, leaving the school staffed with three men who had been associated with him since the beginning of his work. They were all nearly seventy years old. Another problem was lack of funds, along with a declining student body.[8] In spite of the qualifications of the remaining three—Goodrich, Fitch, and Gibbs—the school did not appeal to the young Twichell, active, athletic, and not a deeply serious student.

His good friend, Edward Carrington, moreover, was already enrolled in the Columbia College Law School in New York. Bob Stiles, another classmate and friend, was also planning to be in New York after a year in the South; and Lounsbury was considering such a move. Twichell, therefore, decided on Union Seminary for his divinity work. There seems to be no question about his conscientious purpose in entering upon such study. Like many young men, however, he understandably wanted continued association with his college friends and selected his divinity school more on those grounds than on doctrinal ones. Southington to New Haven to New York—the small-town boy was following a not-unusual pattern.

After spending the summer at home, in the fall of 1859, Twichell and Carrington began rooming together at 108 Waverly Place, Manhattan. A year later Bob Stiles also took rooms there with Lounsbury, who had gone into business for awhile but had found it unpleasant and not particularly profitable. He was then employed in literary work on an encyclopedia. 108 Waverly Place became a meeting place for men of Yale '59, with Date Hannahs coming frequently from Brooklyn, Bill Stiles from Deckertown, and many others dropping in when they were in the city. The friendships that continued through those years were lasting ones.[9]

Political discussions took up much of the time of these recently-graduated Yale men, for it was becoming more and more apparent that war was in the making. As is often true of undergraduates, campus life in New Haven had occupied most of their time and thought for four years. Events in the nation had seemed somewhat irrelevant to them as individuals. Now, away from the self-imposed isolation of campus life, living in New York, they became increasingly concerned with national affairs.

As time passed, the election of Lincoln, the secession of the Southern states, the formation of the Confederacy, the failure of the Peace Congress called by Virginia, all made it evident that the country was approaching a crisis. Stiles, who had spent much of the year after his graduation from Yale in the South, knew that the spirit leading toward war was very strong there, but no matter how he tried to convince his friends that this was true, for a long time the others found it hard to believe.

With the actual outbreak of war, it was necessary for the little group of Yale '59 men to break up. Bob Stiles, born in Georgia, son of a Presbyterian minister, had lived in the North most of the time since he was twelve years old; but his sympathies in the developing conflict were completely with the South. After the firing upon Fort Sumter, he found it impossible to remain in New York, and so he returned to New Haven, where his father and brothers were living, to make plans to go South to join the Confederate forces while it might still be possible to get there.

It was a saddened and very quiet group who accompanied him to the railroad station to bid him farewell on this first lap of the journey that would take him so completely away from them. While they knew and liked him well enough to respect the sincerity of his decision, they regretted deeply the necessity of this kind of parting.

To Twichell, this separation of friends was particularly tragic. Nor was it easy for Stiles to leave his friends. Many years later, Stiles wrote about this group in New York:

> Ed Carrington, a youth of uncommon power and promise, who lost his life during the war in an obscure skirmish in Florida, like myself, was studying law, but he roomed with Joe Twichell, who was then studying theology; dear Joe, who preached the bi-centennial sermon at Yale, and is to-day, as he

has always been, the most admired and best beloved man of the class of '59. My room-mate was Tom Lounsbury. . . .[10]

Until Stiles's departure, it had been easy to consider the national situation mainly as a subject for spirited discussion; but when the other three returned without him to the familiar rooms at 108 Waverly Place, they had little to say. Each one began to think very seriously of his own responsibility in the conflict.

It was not yet a time for definite decisions as to what their contributions would be; but they all knew that they, too, would soon leave as Bob had done, and fight against him. For that is the way it seemed to them then. They would be fighting not against unknown strangers, but, unbelievably, against a good friend.

III

❦

Civil War

ON APRIL 12, 1861, Major Anderson, in charge of the defense of Fort Sumter, received a note from aides representing General Beauregard of the Confederate Army.

It read:

> Fort Sumter, S. C.
> April 12, 1861—3:20 A.M.

Sir:

By authority of Brigadier-General Beauregard, commanding the Provisional Forces of the Confederate States, we have the honor to notify you that he will open the fire of his batteries on Fort Sumter in one hour from this time.

We have the honor to be, very respectfully, your obedient servants,

> James Chesnut, Jr.
> *Aide-de-Camp.*

> Stephen D. Lee
> *Captain, C. S. Army,*
> *Aide-de-Camp.*[1]

On April 14, after thirty-three hours of heavy bombardment, Anderson marched his garrison out, having lost only one man. As the relief ship which was to take them to New York pulled away, the men had what was for many of them their first glimpse of the Stars and Bars, the new Confederate flag, flying from Sumter.

Many people, including Twichell and his Yale friends at 108 Waverly Place, New York, had refused to believe that there would actually be war; but the news of Sumter, followed by the return to New York of Anderson's garrison, left no room for further hope that war might be averted.

19

Soon after Bob Stiles's departure from New York, Twichell
decided to see if he could enlist as a chaplain in the Union Army.
Although not yet ordained, he had completed almost two years
of divinity school. After a quick trip to Southington to discuss
this important decision with his family, he returned to New York
and enrolled as regimental chaplain with the 71st New York
State Infantry, Second Regiment, Excelsior Brigade, which was
then being recruited.[2]

On April 29, 1861, he reported for duty at Camp Scott on
Staten Island, having enlisted for a period of three years. Not
yet twenty-three years old, and with only Southington, Yale, and
the year and a half at Union behind him, he was hardly ready
for the life he was to lead for the next three years. They were,
in some ways, more important than any similar period of time
in his past, however, as preparation for the life ahead of him.
The man he was upon enlistment could hardly, for instance, have
gained the friendship and admiration of Mark Twain. The three
years were to see many significant changes in his attitudes and
outlooks on life. The ideal of service to God and humanity
which had been emphasized at the Lewis Academy, in his home,
and in his church made it seem obvious to him that his personal
desire to complete his divinity studies must be postponed. He did
not feel that this was a necessarily noble or patriotic decision: it
was, simply enough, the only decision.

Never before had he had contact with the kinds of humanity
which made up the 71st New York. Most of the regiment was
recruited from the lowest elements of the New York City streets.
Some of the men had been serving prison sentences on Blackwell's
Island, but were released if they would enlist in the 71st. From
one-half to two-thirds of the recruits were Catholics, but most of
them in name only, not having been inside a church for many
years. Many were of Irish descent and had grown up on the streets
of New York where they had survived only by fighting for existence. When no common enemy was at hand, they fought among
themselves.

Their interest in religion was small. Before a chaplain was
assigned to the regiment, an election was held among the men
to determine what kind of chaplain they preferred. Over 400
voted for a Catholic priest, 154 for any kind of Protestant minister, 11 for a Mormon elder; and the rest indicated that they
wished to have no clergyman at all. Twichell's first ministry was

certainly not going to be with the kind of men he had planned to work with during his educational years.

In his boyhood Twichell had seen the respect accorded Mr. Jones in his Southington parish; he had also witnessed the glamor and excitement surrounding Horace Bushnell with his unorthodox views. Feeling that he did not have the spiritual power of a spectacular man like Bushnell, he had, nevertheless, looked forward to the kind of ministry experienced by Mr. Jones. He had imagined that he would have a small parish, like the one at home, in which to preach on Sunday, marry the young, baptize the babies, bury the dead, perhaps write theological and literary articles, and stroll through the town being greeted by all with respect and friendliness.

His was not necessarily an egotistical approach to the ministry; it was the only one he had known. Evangelical Christianity was beyond the range of his personal experience. So, too, was service to those who did not customarily respect the position of the minister. Even Horace Bushnell was treated respectfully, so far as Twichell knew then, by those who disagreed violently with his views. Yale and Union had done little to change his early outlook, and his closest friends in both places had been young men from backgrounds very much like his own.

He knew that he was joining a rough regiment, however, and did it consciously. He wrote to his father that he had discovered that regiments less difficult were already supplied with chaplains, and he thought himself particularly well-fitted to work with the dregs of society which were going into the 71st. While he *may* have "recognized intuitively that, unlike the paler parson of less adaptable temperament, he could get along with the scourings of the pavement and bring to them a kind of leadership they had never known," it seems more likely that, with his background and limited experience, he was simply filled with the kind of youthful exuberance that made anything seem possible.

Confident that he would have no trouble with the men, he was worried, however, that he might have difficulties with the Brigade Chaplain, who would be, in some respects, his superior officer. Confiding this concern to his father, he wondered what he would do if the Brigade Chaplain turned out to be an Episcopalian! The non-religious he could try to convert to Christianity; those who disagreed with him in doctrine he was almost afraid of. Like his Yankee Puritan forebears, he apparently did not con-

sider tolerance a strength. Congregationalism was the only truth
to him and to many of his contemporaries as it had been at an
earlier time when the first settlers arrived (including his ancestor
Joseph Twichell of the Massachusetts Bay and Connecticut settle-
ments), and to tolerate someone else's views would be completely
impossible, for such tolerance would indicate lack of certainty
about one's own position. This early in his war experience, it
begins to seem evident that much change was to occur before
this comparatively narrow young man could move to Hartford,
accept the leadership of a large church, and enjoy the friendship
of Mark Twain.

For the first few weeks after his arrival at Camp Scott he was
busy with the necessities of securing equipment and getting
located with his regiment. On April 21, eight days before he reported for duty, the first part of the 71st New York had left for
Washington, each man equipped with a rifle, bayonet, cartridge
box, cap, pouch, and blanket. Since their uniforms had not yet
arrived, the men wore civilian clothes of all kinds. Knapsacks
had not been provided as yet, either, and so, valises, boxes, and
bags in hand, the civilian- attired first part of the 71st had marched
off to war looking more like immigrants than soldiers.

By the time the remainder of the 71st left Camp Scott to join
the advance group, the equipment problem had been taken care
of. The five or six weeks they spent on Staten Island before leaving for the South were crucial ones for Twichell. In one respect,
his background may have been helpful; for he probably would
have had no success at all with these men if he had attempted to
start some sort of revival movement. Since that kind of approach
had never occurred to him, anyway, he began slowly to make his
place among the men. For awhile, in Yankee fashion, he said
practically nothing; but he spent much time wandering around,
observing, thinking, waiting until he had the situation clearly in
mind before he decided what to do about it.

One of his first jobs was to convince the officers that he needed
facilities for services. That accomplished, he found that he lacked
men to attend the services. As he moved around the camp every
day he gradually became acquainted with a few men here and
there—some of them, those like himself, somewhat out of place
with the majority. In spite of the reputation of the 71st, there
were many volunteers in it who were not from the dregs of society, and soon they began to appear at his services. Having spent
the winter studying in New York City, Twichell, still young and

athletic and with memories of undergraduate sports activities at Yale, enjoyed being outside in the spring and began to participate in some of the spontaneous sports events of the men during off-duty hours. First offended and upset by the language he heard, he soon found it fruitless to attempt to correct that situation and began to use the sports activities simply for enjoyment and as an opportunity to become acquainted with more men.

After securing a place for services, his next battle with the officers was to get time from the training schedule for Sunday services. It was a hard fight, because the officers found Sunday an excellent day for parades and reviews.

He wrote to his father:

> Because, forsooth, it is a fine day for shows and a grand parade has been ordered. Even while I write, the tramp of regiments, the roll of drums, the resonant brass, the shrill fife, rise upon the air, inspiring, even grand at the proper time, but when intruding upon the hours demanded by God for better purposes, a profanation and a shame. It hurts my Puritan ears to listen. . . . We learn anew that we must assert ourselves.[3]

And assert himself he did, firmly and persistently, until by June he was winning that battle and was conducting services in time allowed by the officers, attempting to minister to Catholics and Protestants alike. The men attended originally, many of them, from amusement; for it must have been amusing to see this young, slender boy preaching to the rough soldiers of the 71st. Word had also gotten around about his battle with the officers for time for these services, and many of the men wanted to see this boy who had had an argument with their officers—and won.

He never touched upon doctrinal matters in this mixed group. His practical sense told him that they would not be interested in such matters, and so he devoted his sermons to the current problems of army life, condemning profanity, stealing, drinking—preaching always the dignity of man. He even had some success; not that sin was much abated, but services were better attended as time went on. His sincerity got through to the men, and he began doing much individual counseling in the time between services and drills. Farther and farther behind him went the Latin, Greek, and formal theology which he had learned.

By the time the 71st moved toward the Potomac in July, the young chaplain had made his place among the officers and the men. He had heard much about the past lives of the soldiers, lives very different from any he had known firsthand before. He had been forced to try to help them look forward to the future, when life might be better for them. This optimism, this hope of future betterment for any who seriously desired it and would work for it, became here a permanent part of his philosophy, something he would emphasize during his whole life when he counseled those in trouble.

During much of August, September, October, and November, the 71st was on the move. Discipline became impossible to maintain; desertions were frequent. The sight of the chaplain struggling along under several packs became a familiar one, because many of the men lacked the stamina for prolonged physical exertion. Years of sub-standard living had weakened them permanently. The officers plainly did not understand his actions in thus assisting the weak. The men came to accept it. Although he "perspired like rain as my Father's son should," he was strong enough to handle the extra exertion easily.[4]

His convictions were unchanged, in spite of the change in his life. While he was not preaching on doctrinal matters, he had not yet varied even slightly from his original Yankee position. Although he found the other officers friendly and occasionally enjoyed their company, he assured his father that he had not, by associating with them, compromised himself as a Christian and clergyman. He also expressed tremendous relief when he found that the Brigade Chaplain was not an Episcopalian, but a Congregationalist like himself, and, to make matters ideal, a Congregationalist from Connecticut, the small town of Winsted which was not particularly near Southington— but it was still Connecticut.

During the fall his main problems were an epidemic of typhoid and continuing regimental difficulties with the men's excessive drinking, problems which concerned him equally. In the field, the drinking problem was aggravated by poor whiskey. Finally, one man from Company H, after forty-eight hours of marching without sleep, obtained some poor whiskey, drank too much of it, was drunk all afternoon, and was found dead in his tent the next morning. To Twichell this was awful, horrible, and he insisted that the whole regiment be gathered for the funeral service at which time, "I spoke my mind freely and I hope in the fear of God. The occasion was one calculated to inspire the preacher and hold the audience. I had the advantage of breathless attention, and I have good reason to believe, that by God's help, my words were not in vain."[5]

On October 5, 1861, another chaplain joined the 71st New York, in addition to Twichell and the Brigade Chaplain. Twichell was not pleased with this event, for his fellow chaplain turned out to be Father Joseph B. O'Hagan, S. J. When the two men were introduced at Brigade headquarters, there was decided coolness on both sides. After all, Twichell had worried about the possibility of being forced to associate with an Episcopalian chaplain. He had not even considered the chance of association with a Catholic chaplain as a probability, and he was very definitely not happy about the situation. Father O'Hagan was likewise displeased, because, knowing in advance that the regiment was predominantly Catholic and that the men had voted to have a priest as chaplain, he had not even known that a Protestant chaplain had already been assigned to the 71st and had been with them for some time.

Throughout the long winter of 1861-1862, which the 71st spent in lower Maryland, there was little activity for either man beyond the normal routine of a chaplain's duties—conducting religious services, helping the men with personal problems, taking trips to Washington with money which the men wanted deposited in banks or sent home.

Of necessity, the two chaplains were thrown together often. The typhoid epidemic raged, and Twichell often had to send for Father O'Hagan when a Catholic soldier desired the last rites of the Church. During the Civil War chaplains were also in a fairly awkward social position regarding rank. Their rank was that of Chaplain, and their names were to appear on the list of officers, but they had no other official military rank and were considered to be neither officers nor enlisted men. For the best performance of their religious duties, this kind of classification was convenient, because they were at home with both officers and men. When not occupied with duties, however, they were still neither one nor the other, and thus were often left to themselves for social companionship.

During the long winter evenings, the two men spent much time together, talking about their past lives. The conversations were at first simply polite and formal. Forced into each other's company, it seemed as if each had decided that he would be a Christian gentleman and make the best of an awkward situation, but he would, of course, not enjoy it.

To Twichell, whose travelling had been sharply limited, Father O'Hagan's past was very interesting. Born in the Parish of Clogher,

County Tyrone, Ireland, on August 15, 1826, he had emigrated as a youth, going to Nova Scotia where his brother lived. After spending some time there on classical studies, he was admitted to the Seminary by Archbishop Walsh of Halifax. Before completing his course of studies for the priesthood there, he spent the summer of 1847 in Boston where he met a Father McElroy who persuaded him to remain in Boston.

In December, 1847, he began his Novitiate in the Society of Jesus, studying Rhetoric, Philosophy, and Theology. In 1852, he began to teach in the old Seminary in Washington, D. C. From 1855 to 1857 he taught at Georgetown College. In the fall of 1857 he went to Belgium for further studies and was ordained there.

He returned to the United States just as the Civil War was beginning. Father Paresce, the Jesuit Provincial in Washington, D. C., decided to appoint him to military service. And so, on October 5, 1861, he had arrived at regimental headquarters of the 71st New York State Infantry.[6] He was at first startled when he realized the kind of men with whom he would be serving, but he, like Twichell a few months earlier, soon made the adjustment and began to see that his services were needed very much by this tremendously heterogeneous group.

The two chaplains gradually began to find that they had much in common. Their early classical educations were much alike, and while neither was primarily interested in scholarship, they both had good educational backgrounds and much material for non-controversial conversation. Carefully they avoided theological discussions in these first few months together except as factual experiences of their past lives.

Soon the stocky Irishman and the tall Yankee began to be seen more and more together, often laughing as they walked and talked, for they had found in each other similar humorous reactions to life in general.

In April, 1862, the 71st began to see its first action when it was assigned to take part in McClellan's Peninsular Campaign. May 5, 1862, was an important day to the regiment and to its two fairly inexperienced chaplains. In the morning the men were in marching order, preparing to move to the front lines to relieve the regiments which had been fighting for many hours and were suffering many casualties. The rain was pouring down, soaking the men, and making the protection of equipment extremely difficult. The fighting was close enough to their lines so that the deafening sounds of the artillery beat continually on their ears. Wounded men from the advance regiments were being carried past the waiting men of the 71st to first aid stations in the rear, increasing the apprehension of the waiting troops. Occasionally, shells burst very close to them.

Father O'Hagan had all the Catholic soldiers step two paces forward, kneel in the mud and repeat an act of contrition. He pronounced the formula of absolution. Without a word being spoken to them, the non-Catholic soldiers had removed their hats and seemed impressed with the scene.

When the orders to advance were given, the two chaplains went ahead with these men with whom they had spent many months. Casualties in the 71st on that one day were approximately five hundred.

Twichell, like the other Protestants in the group, was impressed with the solemnity of the pre-battle scene and also with the sincere devotion of Father O'Hagan. As the battle raged, the two of them dashed among the men, bringing the wounded back to safety, giving comfort to the dying (regardless of their faith) and giving no thought to their own personal safety. By evening the fighting was over, and two very tired chaplains had ahead of them a long night of burying the dead where they had fallen and ministering to the wounded. For Twichell, this first battle experience was almost overwhelming. He said later of this day:

> I shall never forget the time when first I saw the dead lying on the field of battle. It was in 1862 at Williamsburg. Just at sunset I entered the pine wood in which most of that sanguinary engagement was fought. Treading the soft carpet that pines spread at their feet, I wandered through the awful place. There they lay, the uncertain light and sombre shade revealing the marble of their still faces, the low minor-keyed moan of the gentle west wind through the black boughs above droning their dirge, there they lay, my slain countrymen. Young men from Maine and young men from Georgia, boys from Massachusetts and boys from the Carolinas, side by side as the shifting line of battle had left them, sleeping their last sleep now peaceful together, differing only in their garments, their features much alike, all Americans, the sons of mothers still unconscious of bereavement, dead corpses. I was like one in a hideous nightmare. It was a sight too piteous for speech. It seemed as if the universe would stop with the horror of it. I could only cry to my own leaded heart, "It costs too much."[7]

Having pushed themselves to the point of exhaustion, doing the same things, they now had another bond in common. Both chaplains mentioned this one day often in later years. No other experience of their long wartime service made a deeper impression on either of them. No other single experience was to bring them closer together. Four days later, when the 71st, reassembled and reorganized after its great loss of men, moved on to its next assignment, there was no doubt about the relationship between the two chaplains. They had gone through this horrible experience together, and from here on they would be more often together than apart.

Thus, Father O'Hagan became Twichell's first close friend who was not like him in background and doctrine. Joe had taken another step along a path that was leading slowly to Hartford—and to a friendship with Mark Twain, another man who would differ from him radically in doctrine, but who would be a close friend. The possibility of their companionship was becoming greater as Twichell widened his horizons.

Within a few weeks Twichell put some of his thoughts into poetry, poetry which he never publicly claimed as his own. When it finally appeared in print on May 5, 1890, he put it in his scrapbook, along with a notation that he was the author. His name did not accompany the poem in the newspaper.

BURIED ON THE FIELD

(The following verses, never before published, were composed by an officer of the Army of the Potomac on the march up the Peninsula soon after the battle of Williamsburg, which occurred May 5, 1862, twenty-eight years ago to-day.)

They're left behind!
Our steps are turned away:
We forward march, but these forever stay
Halted, till trumpets wake the final day:—
Good-bye! Good-bye!

They're left behind!
The young and strong and brave:
The sighing pines mourn sweetly o'er their grave;
Mute, moving grief the summer branches wave,
Good-bye dear friends!

They're left behind!
Four days we staid to keep
A sacred sentry o'er their glorious sleep:—

The drops of heaven above are left to weep;
          Good-bye! Good-bye!

     They're left behind!
   There let soft sunshine fall
   Thro' tremulous leaves; and where sad night birds call,
O moon and stars! kiss through the shadowy pall,—
          Good-bye! Good-bye!

     They're left behind!
   And fold them to thy breast
   In gentle arms, O soil! now doubly blest
By their live valor and death's noble rest:
          Good-bye! Good-bye!

     They're left behind!
   Comfort!—our heavy souls!
   Their battle shout forever onward rolls
Till God's own freedom gathers in the poles!
          Good-bye! Farewell![8]

On July 8, 1862, Twichell saw President Lincoln for the first time. Accompanied by Secretary Stanton, Lincoln visited the Army of the Potomac while it was resting at Harrison's Landing on the James River, after the fierce Seven Days' Battle. The President's visit was a surprise. As he rode along the lines the soldiers cheered, "but with the feeling [Twichell fancied], 'We are the chaps to be admired. It is you—Abraham and Edwin—that ought to do the cheering!' "

Twichell was particularly interested in the reaction of Ben, the Negro cook whom the regiment had "stolen" out of Maryland the previous winter. Ben had been out getting provisions and when he returned, he was smiling widely and exclaiming to all who would listen, "I'se seed ole Uncle Linkum!"

Ben had told the men of the 71st that before the war he had never heard a white man say anything favorable about Lincoln. According to Twichell, even though Lincoln had been described to the Negroes as a monster,

> . . . the President had attained the reverence due to a benefactor—
> and that without any abolition tracts or teachings. They hardly
> accounted him a real man, but rather as some half-mythical, far-
> off omen of good, which some day would break the clouds above
> them. Simple minds apprehend *persons* rather than *principles*.[9]

When the first Union soldiers arrived near Ben's home, he and his fellow slaves did not think of them as the Union Army, but rather as visible evidence that the benign reign of Lincoln was at hand. It was no wonder that seeing Lincoln himself provided a real thrill for Ben.

Twichell himself was less thrilled and was more amused than impressed with the President's appearance. He wrote to the family at home:

> I have seldom witnessed a more ludicrous sight than our worthy Chief Magistrate presented on horseback yesterday. While I lifted my cap with respect for the man raised up by Providence to rule our troubled times, I quickly lowered it to cover a smile that over-mastered me. McClellan was beside him, short, stout, stiffly erect, sitting his horse like a dragoon, and the contrast between the two was complete.
>
> It did seem as though every moment the President's legs would become entangled with those of the horse he rode, and both come down together; while his arms were apparently liable to similar mishap. That with which he held the rein, in its angles and position, resembled the hind leg of a grasshopper—the hand before, the elbow away back over the horse's tail. The removal of his hat in front of each regiment was also a source of laughter in the style of its execution; the quick trot of the horse making it a feat of some difficulty, while from the same cause his hold on it seemed precarious. I shall remember the picture a long time.

In spite of his amusement at the ridiculous picture which the President made, with one arm resembling the hind leg of a grasshopper, Twichell also seems to have respected him. He had found that Lincoln's popularity in the army was universal. Other leaders might fall into disfavor, but Lincoln retained the confidence and trust of the men. Over and over he had heard officers and men say that as soon as Lincoln knew about some complaint of the moment, all would be corrected. They felt that he would not be easily duped and could be depended on to do the right thing.

Twichell concluded his description of this visit of the President:

> His benignant smile as he passed on was a real reflection of his honest, kindly heart; but deeper, under the surface of that marked and not all uncomely face, were the unmistakable signs of care and anxiety. God bless him and give answer to the prayers for guidance I am sure he offers.[10]

The 71st continued to see much action: Fair Oaks, Malvern Hill, Bristoe Station, Second Bull Run. While on the move, the two chaplains travelled together: Twichell riding his Garry Owen; O'Hagan his St. Cecilia.

During the summer, the two men had to go to Washington. O'Hagan was anxious for this opportunity to return to Georgetown to see his friends and to get away from the horrors and discomforts of war for at least a short time of peace and quiet. Since their leave was not long enough for Twichell to go to Connecticut, Father O'Hagan invited him to accompany him to Georgetown. While the two men had become friendly, Twichell was not at all sure that he wanted to be completely surrounded by Jesuits, and wondered just how startled they might be if he walked casually into their midst; but the thought of warm food, baths, and beds proved to be more powerful than his hesitation because of religious differences.

Off to Georgetown they went, Congregational parson and Jesuit priest, to be accepted with open arms by the Fathers there. For several days they basked in the peace at Georgetown. Twichell was accepted as a friend of O'Hagan's and respected as a man doing an important job with the troops. There was much joking and laughing during the few days, and two very much refreshed clergymen rejoined the 71st.

Twichell's complete acceptance of Father Joseph B. O'Hagan, S. J., was a very important step in his own development and broadening. In less than a year he had moved far from his original narrowness, and primarily because of this one man and their shared experiences. It was fortunate for Twichell's later work that the priest assigned to the 71st was a man like Father O'Hagan. Basically, they seem to have shared an interest in humanity that surpassed their concern with theology. With war and death all around them, they could hardly be disturbed by their doctrinal differences. Perhaps Twichell's statement that simple minds apprehend persons rather than principles might be applied to well-educated minds, also. Persons were very important to both of them, and they could accept each other as a person, neither one changing his religious principles, but both benefiting from a friendly personal relationship. Both had an ever-ready sense of humor, and also a cheerfulness that could survive many blows. They undoubtedly helped to carry each other through some of the worst times in the early years of the war.

In the summer of 1863, they both received their first extended furloughs. In one year Twichell had reached the point where he would visit Georgetown with Father O'Hagan. After two years he was ready to invite him to his home in Southington. He did so with an almost belligerent attitude because he knew he would

shock many of the townspeople. He knew that Connecticut reserve, however, can be an advantage in what might be an awkward
situation because no matter how startled or even disapproving
they are, New Englanders are apt to react with quiet courtesy. If
the people in Southington were shocked, they may have had many
private conversations about the strange situation (and probably
did). Deacon Twichell's eldest son had come home with a friend,
however, and there is a proper way to treat a guest.

People were also anxious to have direct news from the battlefields, and the two chaplains spent many hours telling and retelling of the Peninsular Campaign. When the two left, sincere in-
vitations were offered to Father O'Hagan to return whenever he
could. Reference to him later in the community was usually made
with characteristically meaningful brevity, "Nice fellow."

The winter of 1862-1863 was a miserable one for the 71st. The
battle at Fredericksburg was a bloody one for Federal troops.
While the shock that both Twichell and O'Hagan had felt at
seeing their first battlefield dead at Williamsburg was more powerful than any later experience could be, neither could ever become
callous to the deaths and suffering around them. Their companionship, which by now was a real friendship, was a help to both
of them.

The night after the awful day at Fredericksburg, when both
chaplains had worked among the wounded and dying until the
small hours of the morning, they finally tried to get some rest.
It was December, very cold, and they were both completely exhausted physically and emotionally.

After they had been trying to get to sleep, Father O'Hagan
called, "Joe, are you awake?"

"Yes, what is it?"

"Aren't you cold?"

"Yes, very cold."

"Suppose we club our blankets."

Both got up, made a new bed by putting their blankets together, and lay down again, much more comfortably. Very soon
Twichell began to drop off to sleep, but he realized that Father
O'Hagan was laughing quietly. This seemed very strange to him
after the kind of day they had both had.

"What are you laughing at?" Joe whispered.

"I am laughing at this scene."

"Scene? What scene?"

"The scene of you and me—me, a Jesuit priest, and you, a Puritan minister of the worst kind, spooned together under the same blankets."

Twichell was amused, too. After considering the situation for awhile, they decided that probably the angels liked the sight of it—and went to sleep.[11]

The next few months were spent on the Rappahannock, with the opposing armies facing each other, but with only a few skirmishes. In February Father O'Hagan decided to record his experiences in a diary, which he kept faithfully—for nineteen days. The first part of the month was fairly peaceful, with the chaplains spending their time visiting the wounded and doing other routine matters. The cold and mud and generally unpleasant atmosphere put morale at a low ebb. Occasionally, the men were taken off on some kind of march, the chaplains remaining in camp. On Saturday February 7, the entire regiment returned after a two-and-a-half-day march of forty-five miles, during which time they had succeeded in burning one bridge.

During part of the time that the 71st spent in Virginia, Twichell was quartered in a farmhouse. One amusing incident that occurred there is of importance as an indication of how far he had left Connecticut behind him. In January, 1872, Father O'Hagan told the story in a speech which he delivered in Boston.

The owner of the farm where Twichell was staying was a Mrs. White. According to Father O'Hagan she told Joe that when she saw the Union Army arrive in Virginia all of her greatest fears were realized except one—and that one, which she hoped would never happen, would be to see a Catholic priest in that area.

The next day, Father O'Hagan, whose quarters were uncomfortable, went to the farm to visit his friend Joe and to write some letters. While he was busy writing, Twichell went downstairs and said to Mrs. White, "Who do you think is in my room?"

"I can't imagine," replied the Virginia lady.

"A Catholic priest."

"A Catholic priest in my home," she cried, "in my home? Oh, this is horrible!"

"Yes," said Joe, "a Catholic priest—and writing a letter."

"To whom is he writing?" Mrs. White asked.

"Well, I suppose," replied Twichell, adding disaster to disaster, "to the devil."

"To the devil? And how can he send it?" asked Mrs. White, not sure now how much of this tale she was to believe.

"Well," replied the homesick Yankee parson, "I suppose he'll send it by way of Richmond, because that is the nearest way to the devil that I know."[12]

Father O'Hagan and Twichell enjoyed this episode when it happened, and O'Hagan's delight in retelling it years later was obvious. He probably never realized that it is really a significant anecdote to be told of Twichell so few years after he had dreaded the thought of working with an Episcopalian. The change had been gradual, and he himself seems to have been unaware of it. Not only had he fully accepted O'Hagan as a friend, but now he was making fun of someone who held a position very close to what his own had been a short while before.

In April, 1863, Twichell saw Lincoln for the second time. The officers were invited to General Sickles' headquarters at Fitzhugh House to welcome the chief executive, who had come to visit the troops. Although the distinguished guest arrived two hours late, he was greeted enthusiastically, Twichell noting that an abundant supply of food and drink had kept the waiting officers from becoming restless at the delay.

All had a chance to shake hands with the President, and Twichell thanked him for the Day of Fasting and Prayer that he had recently appointed. Lincoln appeared pale and careworn, but not dispirited.

One incident at the reception amused and impressed Twichell because of its informality. The receiving line had several hundred people in it, waiting to be presented to Lincoln. As the many formal introductions took place, Lincoln looked down the line and recognized an old friend from Illinois. Immediately, the two began signaling to each other. When that officer's turn came for formal introduction, Lincoln grabbed him by the hand and spun him round and round, until they looked like boys playing a game.[13]

In July, 1863, when the Excelsior Brigade arrived at Gettysburg, Twichell seems to have forgotten his original attitude toward the character of the majority of the men in the 71st. They had been together for two years; many had been left behind at Yorktown, Williamsburg, Fair Oaks, Malvern Hill, Bristoe Station, the second Bull Run, Fredericksburg, Chancellorsville. As he watched the battle of Gettysburg begin, he found: "It was upon the Excelsior Brigade that my gaze was fastened, for my heart was there. I find it set down in my journal of that day, that watching it, I said to myself: 'There go the bravest men in this army!' "[14]

Often in later years, after he had been long established in his church in Hartford, Connecticut, newspaper articles mentioning his war service said, mistakenly, that he had served with a Connecticut regiment. All these clippings were placed in his scrapbooks, but whenever the mistake was made, he wrote carefully beside the clipping, "No. 71st N. Y.!"[15]

The problem of desertion was one which disturbed all chaplains. From the beginning of the war, some men had simply deserted and gone home again. As the war went on, however, the large bounties offered to substitute recruits aggravated the situation. Some men who had been fighting throughout the whole war deserted from one outfit only to accept a bounty and enter another regiment. When they were recognized by old companions, they were often caught.[16]

Twichell, too, had experience with this situation. While eating dinner one day, he happened to see Edward Carrington's regiment marching by. He had not seen Ned since they left New York to enter service, so he excused himself from his staff and went to ride along with his old friend. Carrington and his fellow-officers were all unusually quiet and finally explained their mood to Twichell.

One boy in their regiment had deserted to the Confederate Army, then re-deserted back to another regiment of the Union Army. He had arrived in his Confederate greys and expressed the wish to take the oath of allegiance. Not knowing that he had previously served with Federal forces, the officers accepted him. All seemed to be going well, until a soldier from his old company happened to see him. His captain from his first regiment was sent for, entered the room, said, "Hello, Brown," and instantly regretted having indicated this recognition, because he had no desire to have the boy executed. It was too late for retraction, of course, and although no one in the regiment wanted to go through with it, there was no alternative but to sentence the boy to be shot.

Since the regiment had no chaplain, Carrington asked Twichell to see the man. Joe talked to him, prayed with him, and accompanied him to the open grave, where the deserter, kneeling on his own coffin, eyes bandaged, arms tied, asked that a last message be sent to his mother. Twichell promised to deliver the message, then stepped back, and the firing squad was ordered to fire.

Twichell called the boy "as fine a chap as ever you saw." He ended his account of the incident, "Oh, I tell you, war is cruel."[17]

An interesting sidelight of this episode is the fact that during
the time when Twichell was ministering to the boy, he was listed
as AWOL in the records of the 71st. A few days later, an additional entry says, "Absence satisfactorily explained."

During these war years, Twichell came more and more to emphasize the character of the man in his preaching rather than
doctrinal matters. His final wartime theological position may best
be seen in a funeral service which he conducted on the field in
1864. Major Charles H. Owen described this service, calling it one
of the three most impressive religious services which he had witnessed in his lifetime. One of the three, he said, was a High Mass
in St. Peter's, culminating in the Papal benediction; the second
was Gounod's leading his St. Cecilia Mass, on St. Cecilia's Day, in
St. Cecilia's Church; and the third was a funeral service in the
field, conducted by Twichell.

A colonel had been killed in a skirmish. He was a man given
to hasty speech and was not a professing Christian. His life had
been filled with irregularities, but he had been a generous, noble
commander and comrade. When the fatal bullet hit him, he had
literally been damning some men into line to cover others.

Owen described Twichell as dark, tall, graceful, and hardly
more than a boy. He was faced with an extremely controversial
theological situation, for the colonel had had no chance for a
death-bed repentance, and the unpleasant facts of his moral life
were undeniable. Owen himself went to the service with a feeling
of amused curiosity. How would the "boy preacher" deal with this
complex theological issue?

As the service began, Owen was first aware that the preacher's
voice gave no evidence of hesitation, but was firm, clear, confident,
victorious. He recalled that the 71st had heard this voice in time
of battle, and that the wounded had listened to it, nearer and
more subdued.

Writing forty years later, he was still able to remember the
words that had been spoken, a message indicating devotion to the
Master and comradeship with men.

Twichell said:

> I will ask you, my friends, to consider in your hearts what is the
> distinctive feature of the religion of Christ. In what does it most
> differ from and excel all other teachings, all other creeds of proph-
> ets, philosophers or sages? Is it not in the simple appeal to love
> one another? And the highest realization possible to us of that
> chief end of the teaching of Christ we have defined for us in his

words: "Greater love hath no man than this, that he lay down his life for his friends." Now, this our brother in a general sense did that when he enlisted. He laid his life on the altar of his country's need; he set it between the assaults of an enemy and the safety of his friends; he set it for a guard of the institutions which he loved. And again, in a more special manner, he literally lost his life in saving the friends and comrades in his own command. "He that loseth his life shall find it." We must not mourn him, however much we may miss him. We must rejoice in his promotion and, closing our ranks, seek how nearly we may make good the great loss to our nearer battle line . . . .[18]

Gradually, the preacher-to-be was emerging, in speaking ability and in thought. He and Father O'Hagan had been concerned with men's bodies as well as with their souls. They had come to know men of many kinds, and their interest in humanity had been intensified, in spite of doctrinal differences. The broadening experiences of war in its many aspects were preparing the young preacher very well for ministry in a city church, and friendship with business and literary figures.

The three-year term of enlistment of the 71st was up during the spring of 1864, and Twichell's name appears on the Muster-Out Roll of July 30, 1864. Returning to Southington, he knew he was not yet ready to seek a church. As a man he was much more prepared for pastoral duties than he had been three years earlier, but he had never been a devoted scholar, and much of his formal theology had been forgotten on the battlefields. He was by no means ready to pass the examination which would be given by the governing board of a church considering him as its pastor. In the fall he entered Andover Seminary for an additional year of study to prepare him for the ministry.

By the time that spring vacation came, however, he was restless. Studying doctrinal problems was difficult for him after three years of active living. He returned to Southington, took his horse Garry Owen, which had carried him throughout his years in service, and headed south.

He was in Virginia when Lee surrendered, but he felt no exultation, only great relief that the war was actually over. It would be a long time before the wounds healed.

One day after the surrender he was riding along toward Appomattox, when the numbers of recently released Confederate prisoners going the other way became so great that he decided to remain by the side of the road until they had passed. He held his horse's rein and sat on a fence, paying no particular attention to the individuals going past, when he heard his name called.

Looking up, he saw his old friend Bob Stiles standing near him. He had heard nothing from or about Bob since 1861 when Bob had left New York to join the Confederate Army. When Joe and Edward Carrington had met during the war, they had talked about Bob and wondered what had happened to him. The days when the four young Yale '59 men had shared bachelors' quarters in New York seemed long ago. For six years, at Yale and in New York, these men had been good friends.

Into Twichell's mind flashed many happy memories, mixed with the poignant recollection of Stiles' departure when the war started. His first clear thought was relief and pleasure that his friend was still alive. Bob had never been an enemy officer in his mind. Dropping his rein over a post, he rushed through the crowd, both hands extended in greeting. To his dismay, Bob refused to shake hands with him.

Disappointed and annoyed, he asked, "Then why did you call me?"

Bob refused to answer. Twichell asked him if he had heard about Carrington's death, and he nodded. Giving up any hope of friendly conversation, Joe returned to the fence. He was bewildered by Bob's attitude. Peace had come, but had the war really ended?

Some years later the friendship was re-established, and Stiles visited Twichell in Hartford. He said that he had regretted calling to Joe the instant he spoke his name. He did not understand himself why he had then refused to talk.[19]

For the rest of his life, his war experience provided Twichell with various kinds of sermon materials. He was always active in veterans' affairs in Connecticut, as chaplain or other officer.

His only other known venture into poetry came after Lee's surrender. The simple four lines appeared in the Hartford *Courant;* and in his scrapbook, he wrote beside the clipping, merely "April 15, 1865."

The Sad Undertone

> The dead are lying underground.
> Would God that they were here!
> Dear Comrades! O, return of grief!
> To-day ye seem so near.[20]

His friendships with individuals like Stiles he resumed in later years. When he became better known, articles even appeared in

Southern papers, written by Confederate soldiers who remembered his kindnesses to them during the war. But he never completely forgave. As late as 1896, while dedicating a statue to the late President Woolsey of Yale, on the campus, he interrupted his prepared remarks to add:

> And if I may be pardoned, I must say that if it were possible that face would be averted from the scene, when it shall happen this afternoon,—if so be it shall happen—that an ivy from the grave of Robert Lee, a good man, but the historic representative of an infamous cause, shall be planted on this campus to climb the walls of ever loyal Yale.[21]

According to the report in the papers, the older portion of the audience applauded vigorously, but the seniors kept still and looked a little glum.

No other three-year period in his life saw greater changes in the man. In many ways, he was now ready to accept the pastoral responsibilities that would soon be given to him. He was likewise prepared to deal with many men different in background from himself.

The boy who graduated from Yale in 1859 could not have become a friend of or an influence on Mark Twain, nor would he have been the able and well-known preacher that a large church needed.

The man who emerged from three years of a wartime chaplaincy was ready for these and many other things. Although the major part of his life was spent in Connecticut, the three years on the battlefields of the South, with the 71st New York State Infantry (and Father O'Hagan) made him a much broader man than he could have become within the much narrower sphere of his home and educational influences. At the end of the Civil War, he had by no means lost the benefits which he had gained from his boyhood and college years, but he had added many valuable things to his personality, attitudes, and ideas.

Later change and development there may have been, but by the time he left the 71st New York, all the seeds were there in his personality and total outlook that would be brought to fulfillment later.

IV

寒豪

Hartford and the Founding of the Asylum Hill Congregational Church

IN 1865, Twichell, his divinity work at Andover completed, moved to Hartford, a city where he had visited, but where he had few acquaintances and little knowledge of community problems. Like many another young man, he found difficult the transitions from war to school to a responsible position. One of his first tasks was to become acquainted with the kind of city he was entering.

Before the actual outbreak of war, he remembered, Connecticut had not been anxious for Civil War. Its citizens, in general, had preferred colonization of the Negroes, a plan which was being proposed by various factions elsewhere. The North annually sent $100,000,000 worth of goods to the South, and Connecticut, which was becoming highly industrialized, did not want its trade decreased or stopped completely by war.

Even Connecticut agriculturists agreed, since agriculture would be drastically affected by a break with the South. The biggest commercial crop in the state was tobacco, most of which could be used only as cigar wrappers. There would be no profit, the growers well knew, in cigar wrappers if no filler were available from the South.

These were pre-war problems which Twichell's Southington, Yale, Union, and Andover years had given him little knowledge of. Even the attitudes of his fellow students, which had led them to early enlistments after the outbreak of war, were not typical of much of the prevailing mood in Connecticut.

When war came, however, there was no choice for the state but to join in wholeheartedly. On January 17, 1861, Governor William A. Buckingham issued a proclamation to the militia of the state, warning them to be prepared for an emergency. He also ordered the quartermaster to buy equipment for five thousand additional men.

On Monday, April 14, 1861, two days after the firing on Fort Sumter, the Presidential proclamation came for 75,000 troops in three months, Connecticut's quota being one regiment. Since the law did not allow the governor to order the state militia to serve out of the state, volunteers were called for, and three regiments were quickly formed.

In the office of the Hartford *Press*, Joseph R. Hawley, the editor, and later to become one of Twichell's parishioners, with Albert W. Drake and Joseph Perkins, volunteered. By nightfall the company was full. Hawley became first lieutenant, then captain, later lieutenant-colonel of the Seventh Connecticut Regiment, and, finally, brigadier-general.

The assistant editor of the paper, Charles Dudley Warner, later to be one of Twichell's close friends, was prevented from volunteering by poor eyesight. Since General Hawley, after the war, continued in public life as Governor of Connecticut and member of Congress in both branches, the assistant editor continued to be in charge of this influential paper, except for a short period immediately after the war when he and Hawley were part-proprietors. When the owners of the *Press* purchased the century-old *Courant*, Warner continued as editor of the combined papers.

Thus, while Twichell was with the 71st New York, the Hartford he was to know and the friends he was to make were gradually becoming established in the positions in which he would find them.

The other Hartford newspaper also made its contribution to the war. Gideon Welles, born in Glastonbury, was called from his editorial position on the Hartford *Times* to be Lincoln's Secretary of the Navy. He presided over the formation of an effective Navy and directed the blockade of the South which hastened the end of the war.

Not including indirect loss or private contributions, the expense of the war to Connecticut was more than six and a half million dollars. Of a population of 461,000 (80,000 voters), 54,882 men were in the national service. There were twenty-eight regiments of infantry, two regiments and three batteries of artillery, one regiment and one squadron of cavalry.

Connecticut suffered casualties of 20,573 men killed, wounded, missing, and dying of disease (209 being officers).[1] Thus had Hartford and Connecticut been affected by the war which had molded much of Twichell's developing personality. Of greater immediate concern to him, however, was the Hartford of 1865. Its past was important, but what of its present?

The city he was to come to know well had grown very rapidly in the last three-quarters of a century. Population figures indicate its growth: 1790—4,090; 1830—9,789; 1850—17,966; 1860—29,152; 1870—37,743. New businesses had sprung up rapidly. As Mark Twain put it humorously in 1874, Hartford was a city capable of taking care of most emergencies, " . . . a city whose fame as an insurance center . . . has given us the name of being a quadruple band of brothers working sweetly in hand, the Colt's arms company making the destruction of our race easy and convenient, our life insurance citizens paying for the victims when they pass away, Mr. Batterson perpetuating their memory with his stately monuments, and our fire insurance comrades taking care of their hereafter."[2]

There were other businesses, also, which interested a newcomer to the city, many of them firmly established by the time that Twichell arrived and surviving to the present. As early as 1846, General Zachary Taylor had written to Samuel Colt, in Hartford, "Send me 1,000 Colt Revolvers at once." To small companies around the state Colt's sublet orders for parts that were assembled at the plant in Hartford, one of the first stirrings of mass production methods.[3]

In 1860, Francis A. Pratt and Amos Whitney opened a one-room shop on Potter Street for the manufacturing of machine tools. By the time that Pratt and Whitney was incorporated in 1869, aid had been secured by the founders from French and British scientists, and a United States Standard Yard had been designated. A gauge department resulted from this research, and precision to the 1,000,000th of an inch was possible.

By the time Twichell arrived at Asylum Hill, Hartford's insurance companies, many of whose executives and employees would be his parishioners, were also well established, the first claim on life insurance having been paid by the Connecticut Mutual to the estate of Dr. William Barry in 1847. The Aetna Life Company was incorporated in 1853; the Phoenix Mutual in 1851, the Connecticut General Life Insurance Company in 1865; and America's first accident insurance company, the Travelers, in 1865.

With these companies and others, Hartford was a busy city. The port was still active on the Connecticut River, although the railroad was now getting much of the business. The most active part of the city was still near the river, and the small towns along the river were becoming more and more closely connected with the city itself.

Running into the Connecticut was a smaller river which Twichell would come to know well, the name of which has never been satisfactorily established so far as local residents are concerned. Although it has long been known to all in the vicinity as the Hog River, it appears on maps as the Park River. At Nook Farm, in the western part of the city, the beginnings of a small community were appearing near this river. It would not be long before Mark Twain would place a row-boat-sized side-wheeler there for the entertainment of the neighborhood boys. Creating a whole group of Huck Finns right in Hartford, Mark and Joe would watch gleefully while the boat was being stolen. When the youngsters returned the boat, Twain would often appear on the balcony just as they were leaving—but the boys were never captured. (It was only when the boys grew up that they realized that Twain had put the little boat there so that it could be "stolen.")[4]

To Twichell, this growing city was soon to become a permanent home. Men from these industries, particularly the executives, were to be members of his church. Residents of the Nook Farm area were to be his closest friends. In this city he was to spend the rest of his life as minister to one church. Here his family of nine children would be born and remain until they left for college. Here he would devote many hours to the problems of people living in a city bursting into life as a business center.

By 1860, the residential area of Hartford stretched several miles from the center, particularly west, up Asylum Hill. On this hill, west of the railroad tracks, many parents found it almost impossible to get their children to Sunday School during the winter months. In November, 1860, therefore, Calvin Stowe started a Sunday School at his home for the children of residents of the area.

It turned out to be a popular and much-needed venture, and since the whole family, as well as the children, were kept from attending church services by the distance and the weather, soon a weekly prayer meeting was started.

This situation continued for several years, though there was much feeling that a new church should be founded. Finally, on February 3, 1864, seventeen citizens of the area met at the American Asylum—with Mr. A. G. Hammond presiding and Mr. Erastus Collins explaining the purpose of the meeting—to consider the needs of the locality, with a view to establishing a Congregational church on the Hill.[5]

Although the seventeen were united in believing that the time had come to create a new religious society, they wished to proceed cautiously. They desired, first, to have the advice of existing Congregational churches in the city. After this first meeting they wrote letters to these churches. All responded promptly by appointing delegates to a later meeting.

On February 6, 1864, another meeting was held, and a resolution was adopted declaring that a new church was needed in the western part of the city. On February 19, Samuel Coit, Erastus Collins, and A. M. Hurlburt were appointed a committee of three to solicit subscriptions, buy a lot, and build a church. Most of these men were business men who were accustomed to large-scale planning. They were also men who acted quickly in an emergency and were used to dealing with large sums of money. The best example of the quick, large-scale business efficiency of these men came later, at the time of the Chicago fire; but it serves now to illustrate the character of the kind of people involved in the establishment of a new church.

In 1871, the Phoenix, for example, had over $1,900,000 in solid assets. When news of the disastrous fire in Chicago reached Marshall Jewell, one of Twichell's parishioners and a large stockholder and director of the company, he hurried from Detroit, where he happened to be visiting, to Chicago. The city was in despair. Jewell met E. J. Bassett of the Aetna, and they decided to take action immediately.

On October 13, they stood near the river, overlooking the destruction of the city. The crowd was milling around near them pointlessly, looking in astonished horror at the rubble, symbol of their tremendous financial losses. The people were close to panic.

Jewell, with no great display, stood on a dry goods box and announced that the Phoenix of Hartford would pay all losses in full, covered by their active policies, and volunteered to pay immediately any claim approved by H. M. Magill, general agent of the western department, who had joined him. The first policy presented was number 10,752, held by Isaac C. Day, for $10,000. Jewell immediately made out a company check—less the interest for two months, the time allowed by the terms of the policy for payment!

Shortly thereafter the Chicago *Tribune* hung a placard from a window announcing that the Phoenix was paying its losses in full. According to the reports, the crowds cheered, and an atmosphere of hope began to replace some of the despair. Near Jewell, Bassett of the Aetna made a similar payment for $7,350 to John B. Drake.

Boston also had a serious fire in 1871, but Hartford insurance companies took the greatest financial loss. The Hartford, Aetna, and Phoenix Insurance Companies paid to policy-holders in Chicago and Boston, $9,162,765.73. Payments of other companies brought the total from Hartford companies to over $12,000,000— from a city of only 38,000 population. The profits in the next few years made good much of the loss, however, and Hartford was firmly established as an insurance center. The quick action on the part of the men involved had built well for the future of the city.[6]

It was men from these companies, and others like them, used to large transactions, quick decisions, and plans for the future, who were involved in 1864 in the founding of a church. It was, perhaps, inevitable that they would treat the church enterprise with similar courage, efficiency, and foresight.

Later, Mark Twain would call their church, the "Church of the Holy Speculators," a description more appropriate than he may have intended; because the founding of a church is in itself a speculation, not only in money invested, but in faith. Could the city support another large Congregational Church? Would the city continue to grow toward the Hill area, so that there would be a residential area large enough to create a congregation over the years ahead? Would people still be interested in later years? Would, perhaps, the city's businesses eventually smother a church in that location?

Certainly, speculators in faith were needed. That these men were accustomed to handling large sums of money and planning far ahead was to their advantage. They took a well-calculated risk as they proceeded with their plans, and the modern visitor to their church can pay tribute to their foresight. The original building still serves its community.

To continue gradually with their progress—in April, meetings were held by representatives of the other churches, approving the organization of the new church. On June 25, 1864, at a meeting held in the West Middle School, the Asylum Hill Ecclesiastical Society was formed, articles of association were signed, and a building committee was appointed. On June 29, the committee on site reported. On July 13, the building committee reported that plans were being prepared. The site committee reported the purchase of land at a cost of $10,000, a joint note being given to the Society of Savings for that amount.

The first public religious service was held on March 12, 1865, in the chapel. On March 23, the church was formed in the ancient New England method by formally accepting a creed and covenant which had been previously prepared. Other churches sent formal recognition and friendly greetings during the next few weeks.

The membership at organization was 114 people, drawn mostly from the membership of other Congregational churches in the city: from Center, 40; from North, 33; Pearl Street, 25; Fourth, 4; South, 2; out of the city, 10.

On May 5, 1865, the cornerstone of the church building was laid. The community could see the speculation in faith take hold as the large Gothic structure was constructed. For 114 members, they were building a church with a seating capacity of 930.

It is obvious that these Hartford business men had proceeded very efficiently in the establishing of a church. $10,000 for the land alone was a sizeable amount of money in 1864. In a period of thirteen months, the church ecclesiastical society had been founded, the chapel built, the church construction started, the membership formed, and fellowship with other churches established. Purchasing land, hiring an architect and builders, raising money, arranging for a mortgage—all these matters were familiar to the "Holy Speculators" of Asylum Hill.

With their organization this far along, however, they could not postpone much longer another important matter, the selection of a minister. And here they hesitated, faltered, disagreed, and, finally, had to seek help. There were questions which they could not answer, because here they had no comparative experience.

Should a new church have a young minister who would grow with it, who would have the enthusiasm and strength to see the church through its early years? Many of the more cautious business men felt that an experienced preacher, familiar with all the aspects of church life, would be a better risk. They knew the value of hiring experienced employees in their companies. Even if they could decide on this and equally puzzling issues, however, where could they find the man they wanted? They knew how to find an architect and hire him to do a particular job; but how to locate and hire a minister was outside the scope of their normal business activities. It *was* within their experience, of course, to seek help from an expert adviser. They knew how to hire specialists and consultants for various responsibilities in their companies.

They turned to Dr. Horace Bushnell, retired minister of the

North Church. Some of them had been members of his church, and all of them were aware of his vast and varied experiences in the ministry. Bushnell was very much pleased that they had come to him, and he recognized immediately the problems that they were facing.

After giving the matter some thought, he felt that he had the answer for them. During the war, a young chaplain on leave and visiting in the city had been introduced to him. In a few days, the two men had seen much of each other. It seemed to Dr. Bushnell that this forthright young man, in spite of his lack of experience, would be quite capable of building a church in western Hartford and of holding his own in dealing with his parishioners, for even then he had acquired the characteristics that made men often describe him as a "man's man."

After meeting and talking with him, the society agreed with Dr. Bushnell's choice; and on June 15, 1865, a letter was written to the Rev. Mr. Joseph Hopkins Twichell of Southington, inviting him to become pastor of the new Asylum Hill Congregational Church.

Twichell's leaves during the war had determined his future life in several ways. The time spent in Hartford, and the meeting with Dr. Bushnell, gave him a church. Another leave he had spent in New York City, where his Yale '59 friend "Date" Cushman Hannahs had introduced him to his cousin, Harmony Cushman. Now that his future seemed to be secure, he could think of marriage.

On November 1, 1865, in Orange, New Jersey, Twichell and Harmony Cushman were married by the Rev. Henry Hopkins. Harmony had been born in Exeter, New York, on August 9, 1843, the daughter of David S. and Julia Curtis Cushman.

On December 13, 1865, Twichell was installed as the pastor of the Asylum Hill Congregational Church in its newly completed chapel. The installation sermon was preached by the Rev. E. C. Jones, Twichell's old pastor from Southington, who had inspired many of his boys to become preachers. The charge to the people was given by Bushnell, the man who had impressed the boy Twichell and his father when they heard him preach in Plainville many years before, and who had recommended him to the people of the new church. He knew that some of them were still a little concerned about Twichell's youth, and he told them that they were lucky not to have a middle-aged man whom they could only watch "running down," but were fortunate in having a young man

whom they could have the pleasure of watching grow up with
them, and that the manner in which he was treated by his congregation would have much to do with his growth.[7]

According to the church records, only a few examinations had
been given to the new minister, and he had passed them well
enough so that the council had recommended him with much
confidence and gratification.

The rumor was, however, that he had had to answer very few
questions, because Bushnell had gotten into a theological argument with one of the other men on the committee, and Twichell
had almost been forgotten. No longer seriously viewed by many
as a heretic, the independent thinker Bushnell could still start
many a controversy. In fact, Twichell himself had been so much
interested at being present at such a discussion with Bushnell that
he had almost forgotten that the meeting had been called to determine his professional fitness for the position. He had, indeed, been
asked very little. In his own scrapbook, which contains a clipping
mentioning the "few examinations," Twichell underlined the two
words firmly.

Soon after his installation, Twichell discovered that his old
companion, Father O'Hagan, now President of Holy Cross College
in Worcester, Massachusetts, was to be in Hartford on church
business. Living in a new place, handling much responsibility,
having little time for personal pleasure, Twichell was very much
excited about the opportunity to relax with a wartime friend,
particularly such a delightful one. The Twichells wrote at once
to invite O'Hagan to stay with them while he was in Hartford.
Father O'Hagan was delighted, accepted at once, and notified the
Catholic Church officials in Hartford that he would not need ac-
commodations, because he was staying in the Congregational
parsonage.

O'Hagan arrived full of enthusiasm at seeing his old friend
Joe, meeting his wife, and seeing the home they had established.
During a long evening, the two men kept Harmony entertained
for hours by telling her about the most delightful aspects of their
war experiences. They had not forgotten the serious and tragic
things that had happened, but this was an evening for happy
memories.

Father O'Hagan wanted to see the new church, too. Much of
the inside of the building had been completed, though the front
was still covered with scaffolding. Leaving Twichell's side on their
tour of the building, O'Hagan scrambled up into this scaffolding,

and on up to the top. He chanted something in Latin, climbed down again, and rejoined Twichell, saying, "Well, Joe, you're going to have a good church. It's been consecrated."[8]

After two years of planning and working, one phase of the holy speculation came to fulfillment with the dedication of the Asylum Hill Congregational Church on June 15, 1866. The church building and furnishings cost $106,208.58, which, in addition to the cost of the lot, made the total cost of church property, $116,208.58—a significant sum for that, or any other, time. The architect was Patrick C. Keely of Brooklyn, New York, who had designed many other churches. The building was a large one, the audience room being 68 by 112 feet, with 186 pews, seating 930 people. The chapel, which had been finished earlier and where services were held until the sanctuary was finished, was 65 by 42 feet, seating 350.[9] The men making the plans had seen far into the future to build this size structure for 114 members, but their speculation proved to be accurate, and Hartford grew as they had thought it would.

Charles Dudley Warner described the Gothic structure of the Asylum Hill Church in his *Backlog Studies*. Recognizing its beauty, he was more aware of the problems which the design of the church created. He felt that his seat was a good one for reflection. He could not see anything because of a large stone pillar in front of him. He could not hear anything because the preacher's voice seemed to wander around in the arches overhead. He said he could recognize the minister's voice because he was a friend of his, but he could not hear anything he was saying.

> When we put him away off in the apse, and set him up for a Goth, and then seat ourselves at a distance, scattered about among the pillars, the whole thing seems to me a trifle unnatural.

There were other difficulties which had to be solved during the first few months that the church auditorium was in use. If the organ were to be placed in the loft, it would hide the rose window. If the choir were up in the loft, like a cage of birds, congregational singing would be hampered. For these reasons, the organ loft was left vacant. Since there was no organ, a melodeon, or cabinet organ, was used, which somehow did not fit the splendor of such a glorious Gothic edifice.

Because the minister could not be heard in many parts of the auditorium, a sounding board shaped like a large shell was placed behind him, but if he moved out of focus, the echoes began.

Next, according to Warner, they moved the sounding board farther back and put the choir, melodeon and minister all in front of it. At the next service they were delighted to find that the appearance of this arrangement was good, and the choir could be heard clearly. When Twichell began to speak, however, very few could hear him because his voice had gone back with the sounding board.

Another proposal, suggested jokingly, was to replace the sounding board behind the minister where it had worked successfully, and place the choir behind it. The singers would be invisible, perhaps giving the effect of an "angel choir."

One construction problem also remained. The building of a spire had been left until later, and, now that the rest of the building was completed, decisions about the design and construction of the spire had to be made.

> If the stranger noticed any lack about our church, it would be that of a spire. There is a place for one; indeed, it was begun, and then the builders seem to have stopped, with the notion that it would grow itself from such a good root. . . . I doubt if it would be in the Gothic spirit to finish a church at once. We can tell cavillers that we shall have a spire at the proper time, and not a minute before. It may depend a little upon what the Baptists do, who are to build near us. I, for one, think we had better wait and see how high the Baptist spire is before we run ours up.

Warner concluded his essay about the new church by saying, "It is needless to explain that a Gothic religious life is not an idle one."[10]

No one was more amused by Warner's discussion than Twichell, who had been with him when many of the choicest bits of description occurred to him, and who had even contributed some of them.

The problems pointed out, however, were real and were serious. The fact that the congregation went at their solution without dismay and with a good deal of humor was, undoubtedly, due to the spirit of their minister. He had preached, certainly, under worse conditions than in this really beautiful Gothic church, and he knew that the problems could be solved. For several months the choir might be found in a different place each Sunday as various experiments were conducted as to where both minister and choir could be placed and heard. Visiting ministers were

sometimes confused by the sounding board, but were warned not to move out of range.

The final addition of the organ made a decided improvement. It was put in the apse; the pulpit was moved forward; the organ enclosed. The congregation could then hear from all parts of the auditorium. When not away on state business, or insurance business as in the instance of the Chicago fire, Governor Jewell stood beside the organist and led the singing.

Within a few years, the worst of the physical problems had been solved. Almost all of the congregation could hear the minister; never would some of them be able to see him if they sat behind the stone pillars.

By 1872, newspapers in many eastern cities were sending reporters to Hartford to attend the Sunday service at the Asylum Hill Congregational Church, and to report on the building, the service, and the dignitaries there gathered.

In regular attendance were many public and literary figures: Governor Jewell; Francis Gillette, who had missed being elected Governor by 40,000 votes; Judge Carpenter, of the Superior Court, who had a Bible class for men; J. Hammond Trumbull, the Indian scholar; Rose Terry, noted New England author; Charles Dudley Warner, editor of the *Courant* and rapidly becoming well known as a humorous essayist; the Chinese students who were in Hartford to attend school, sponsored by their own government; ex-Governor Joseph R. Hawley; occasionally Harriet Beecher Stowe; and, regularly, the Clemens family.

It was not until 1875 that the "stump-tailed" appearance of the church was remedied, when Mr. Roland Mather gave $20,000 to the church for the construction of a spire.

Thus, in a few years after its founding, Twichell's church had grown to be one of the most active in the city, drawing a large congregation every Sunday, with many of Connecticut's leading citizens counted among its members. His meeting with Dr. Bushnell, which had occurred during his wartime leave in Hartford, had proved to be one of the most important events in Twichell's life. He had the ability to build and keep a large membership in a city church, and he was fortunate to have the opportunity to step into such a pastorate immediately upon completion of his year's refresher course at Andover.

Twichell's ability to get along with many different kinds of people apparently helped him with his early parishioners, because in spite of the many difficulties that the new church society had to face, they did so without any serious misunderstandings or disagreements. Twichell's abundant exuberance and good humor eased over many of the problems of those early years. Never reluctant to ask for help or to accept advice, he was able to keep matters running smoothly. The Gothic building was beautiful; its expense had been tremendous; its problems could be solved.

These early years in Hartford also saw the birth of the first two of his nine children, all of whom were to survive him. The first was Edward Carrington Twichell, born August 10, 1868. The second child was a girl, born in 1869, and named Julia Curtis Twichell, for Mrs. Twichell's mother, Julia Curtis Cushman.

Twichell was thus early established in Hartford, where he was to spend the rest of his life. His church society was firmly founded; the church building was beautifully, but perhaps inconveniently, built; and he had a good beginning in winning the respect, admiration, and love of his new parishioners. His home was also firmly established. His relationship with his wife was to be excellent for the remainder of their lives; their home was to be a busy one, with their own nine children, and others whom they took in from time to time to help friends and relatives. The parsonage was at 125 Woodland Street, only a few blocks from the church, and within a few years many well-known and less well-known people would find it an excellent place to visit.

V

※

Theology

UNTIL HE ACCEPTED the pastorate of the Asylum Hill Congregational Church, Twichell had not been forced to enter into
much theological controversy. While he and Father O'Hagan had
undoubtedly differed greatly in doctrinal beliefs, they had been
primarily concerned during the war with their service to the
soldiers. Since they both had great humanitarian interests, they
had put theological differences aside, and friendship had been
strong enough to keep them from wrangling. Conversations they
had had about their differing beliefs had been carried on in a
spirit of friendly curiosity, with neither trying to change the
other's position.

Arriving in Connecticut in 1865, however, Twichell found
himself in the midst of Hartford's greatest doctrinal crisis of the
century. Prior to his arrival, he had known Dr. Horace Bushnell
only as a man and as a prominent, well-known preacher. He had
been aware of the charges of heresy laid against Bushnell, but
he had paid little attention to them. He had read none of Bushnell's published works and had no first-hand knowledge of the
controversy beyond vague memories of discussions in Southington
when he was a boy. Now he found that he had to "take sides,"
because the Congregational churches of the city were still in the
midst of hot discussions, although the peak of controversy had
passed some years before.

Since the men who had had the task of locating a minister for
the new church had gone to Bushnell for assistance, it seemed
that their sympathies must have lain in that direction. Some of
the "few questions" asked at Twichell's examination for the
position indicated that there was some disagreement among these
men, however. It was obvious that the new pastor must come to

know where he stood regarding problems which at the beginning he could not even state.

Twichell himself said: "I came afterwards . . . to comprehend what were the points of his distinctive theology, which I may remark, seemed to me at first all wrong, because it did not agree with what I had before received."[1] Although this realization seemed surprising to Twichell, it was not a really unusual feeling for a young preacher with Yale, Union, and Andover behind him, as may be seen when it is known just what a turmoil Bushnell's theology had created during the previous twenty years.

Bushnell himself was an outspoken man who had never hesitated to preach his own interpretations of theological matters. He had even, in the heat of sincere enthusiasm, been known to be at least slightly rash in some minor matters—as, for example, when he preached on one occasion that our earthly occupations would be continued in the next life and had greatly disturbed an undertaker who foresaw his occupation gone, and a hard-worked elderly lady who had been looking forward to some rest! But on important matters, he had remained clear and consistent, working out a theology satisfactory in the intellectual terms of the nineteenth century, just as Jonathan Edwards had done in the eighteenth century.

Much of Bushnell's doctrine appeared in his collected sermons: *Christ and His Salvation, Sermons on Living Subjects,* and *Sermons for the New Life.* The controversy had not arisen on the basis of these sermons, however; for, taken one at a time, his views apparently did not arouse much excitement. When he came to write his complete theological analyses, however, the storm broke. *God in Christ, Christian Nurture, Vicarious Sacrifice,* and *Nature and the Supernatural* were the most important of these works, and when each was published, editorials and pamphlets followed immediately, warning the faithful of the danger of these heretical views and calling for attacks on such thought.

From early youth Bushnell had been out of sympathy with the current theology and had determined to examine the basic Christian doctrines in terms of logic and reason, as his century understood them. One of the bases for his beliefs was his feeling that language was not a perfect transmitter of Christian doctrine. He felt that the multiplicity of sects had, in good part, been caused by faulty use of language, which he saw only as a sign and image of the truth, and not equivalent to it. On this foundation, he built his theology.

Summed up, this theology disagreed with three basic Calvinistic propositions, the first of which concerned the means by which an individual became a true Christian. Here he disagreed with three basic tenets of Calvinism: total depravity, unconditional election, and prevenient and irresistible grace. These doctrines, he felt, had done more harm than good to mankind, since they demanded that each person must experience some kind of miraculous conversion. In applying human logic to the problem, Bushnell felt that this interpretation of the means of becoming a Christian led only to hypocrisy. His answer he published in *Christian Nurture* in 1846.

He believed that a child became a Christian by living in a Christian home in which he was treated with wisdom and love, and where he had before him continually the best kind of Christian living. Nurtured in this kind of atmosphere, his becoming a Christian himself would not be a sudden or miraculous occurrence; rather, he would grow up never feeling that he had been other than a Christian.

This theory, of course, pointed to a complete revision of child education in the home, school, and church. It was so completely different from current belief that a storm of disagreement was inevitable. Congregationalism would not give up its belief in total depravity easily, nor would it agree to such an easy entrance into the Christian life. In response to this latter charge, Bushnell replied that it was not an easy way; it was very difficult, because it placed such tremendous responsibility on parents, preachers, and teachers of the young to teach them correctly, and also to be in their own lives the best kind of examples of Christian living for the children to observe. That a person might become a Christian by education rather than by a sovereign act of God seemed to the orthodox almost to defy the omnipotence of God.

His second "heretical" view was just as stirring to the orthodox as that expressed in *Christian Nurture,* though it involved a matter which would not necessarily change the way a man behaved in his everyday life. This was expressed in *God in Christ,* where he analyzed the nature of the Trinity. He felt that knowing and understanding the interior being of God and how it was composed was a matter beyond human comprehension. Part of man's limitation as man was an inability to grasp completely a concept of divinity. Believing, then, in one God, a unity, he said that because of man's limited human intellectual capacity, God had revealed himself in the Scriptures as a trinity of persons so that man could better understand the different aspects of divinity. Thus, in the Bible, God as Father, Son, and Holy Ghost was revealed, but, actually. Father, Son, and Holy Ghost were *not* three distinct consciousnesses, wills, and understandings. Instead, they were "instrumentally three,—three simply as related to our finite apprehension, and the communication of God's incommunicable nature."[2]

In so far as it brought the wrath of the orthodox upon his head, this theory of the Trinity was as important as that of Christian nurture. As an influence on the future course of Congregationalism, however, it assumed less significance in a later century when theological speculation is not considered as important to many people as it was in the mid-nineteenth century.

Bushnell's third "heresy" involved the doctrine of the atonement, which provided for partial atonement of some of man's innate depravity by Christ's sacrifice. According to Bushnell, the purpose of Christ's sacrificial death was not that of atoning for man's sin, but was, instead, an example set before man of God's law and character, and would affect the individual man only if he allowed himself to be influenced by the example which Christ had thus portrayed of the spirit of God. In *Vicarious Sacrifice* he stated that wherever love exists, vicarious sacrifice exists also, not as a debt paid, but as a universal and Christian aspect of love.

These three doctrines of Bushnell's: Christian nurture, the nature of the Trinity, and the purpose of Christ's sacrifice not as that of atonement, brought cries of heresy, loud and for a long time undying. The *New York Evangelist* and the *Princeton Review* joined the attack, demanding that Bushnell be presented for trial on formal charges of heresy before the Hartford Central Association. When this was not done, the association of "Fairfield West" urged in 1850 that he be brought before the General Association of Connecticut. In 1850 and 1852 the matter was actually presented before that association, but they did not take action.[3]

The reasons for this lack of action in spite of pressing demands are difficult to determine. Bushnell did have strong friends who upheld his right to speak freely (whether or not they agreed with him); among them was Dr. Noah Porter, later President of Yale University. His own church in Hartford was also firmly behind him. The matter could be brought to the local consocation at any time, however, and trial required, if three members of his own church should complain. Since it might not be impossible to find three dissenters in any large congregation, the church voted to withdraw from the Hartford North Consociation on June 27, 1852. From that time on there was no further danger of trial and that kind of scandal, but the matter did not rest there.

Dr. Bushnell's church, the North Congregational, for many years thereafter stood alone in Hartford, separated in spirit and in actuality from the other Congregational churches in the community. None of the other Congregational ministers would exchange pulpits with him, a custom then prevalent, and none would work with him on any projects of a general Christian or, perhaps, civic nature. For a time, indeed, he had only two personal friends among the clergy of Hartford, because personalities had become so closely tied with doctrine that the other ministers preferred to avoid him completely, socially as well as professionally. Dr. Murdoch of South Baptist Church and the Rev. Thomas M. Clark, rector of Christ Church (Episcopal) were loyal to the man, while disagreeing with his doctrines.

Gradually, the tension lessened, but for a long time there was always the danger of an outbreak. In 1860, the twenty-three-year-old Edwin Pond Parker, later to become one of Twichell's close friends in the ministry, arrived in Hartford to become the pastor of Second Congregational Church. Unfamiliar with Connecticut's theological controversies, he found his examinations perplexing because of the searching questions asked him about the Trinity, inspiration, and depravity. Finally, driven to confusion by the nature of the unexpected questions, when he inadvertently stated that he thought that "God would give every man *a fair chance!*" he touched off another battle which raged for some time in pamphlets and periodicals. Not even realizing at first that he had started this war only because he sounded suspiciously like Dr. Bushnell, he was relieved, he said in later years, when he found that "his little soul was not in great peril among these theological lions, since they much preferred to devour each the other."[4]

Since this conflict had broken out again on the basis of Parker's examination in 1860, it was in full bloom during the years that Twichell was spending on the battlefield. It is not surprising that he knew little about it; because, as was seen, he had been immediately concerned with non-doctrinal matters.

Forced to find out the facts of the controversy after his arrival in Hartford, Twichell was soon convinced by a study of Bushnell's beliefs that here was a theology more satisfactory to his own mind and spirit than any which he had studied previously. Although he was never an original theologian himself, he was an honest thinker, and the rationale of Bushnell's theories appealed to the logic of his own mind.

In his own sermon on the battlefield when the colonel had been killed, Twichell had had to use his own thought to adapt his previous theological education to the circumstances of the moment. His logic then had told him that the colonel would not be condemned to an eternity of punishment when he had served his country and his fellow soldiers so well, and Twichell had preached his funeral sermon with that basic assumption, which was not completely justified by anything that he had learned in divinity studies. Now he found in Bushnell's thought a logical pattern of ideas which he could accept intellectually and emotionally. He adopted Bushnell's theology almost in its entirety.

His admiration of the man and his beliefs, Twichell illustrated in a sermon which he preached after Bushnell's death. He said:

> And so, when at last his days were numbered died Horace Bushnell, the like of whom we shall not see again on earth, but whom through the grace of God we may hope to meet in heaven. The true story of the man cannot be told without the story of his faith. That *is* his story. What he was, he was by reason of what he believed. Oh, may such believing be ours! May Christ in like manner be made our salvation. May that faith, so remarkable alike in its circumstances, and in its quality, so reasonable, so sufficient, so triumphant, be to us a sign that shall not have been given us in vain.[5]

Twichell himself wrote very little theological material, but the few articles he did write were in complete sympathy with Bushnell's views. In an essay called "The Religious Experiences of Childhood," he really merely elaborated some of Bushnell's views expressed in *Christian Nurture,* showing how the Christian personality is developed throughout the childhood years in the home and in the church.[6]

Twichell's own theological contribution, however, was greater than this would seem to imply. Arriving in Hartford in 1865, he found two other comparatively young men in two of Hartford's Congregational churches: the Rev. Nathaniel J. Burton at Fourth Church, and the Rev. Edwin Pond Parker at Second. Very quickly the three became friends and spent much time together. That the friendship was professional as well as social may be seen in the fact that in 1877 they edited a hymnal together, which was published in Hartford by Brown and Gross.[7] The name which Twichell gave to his sixth child, perhaps symbolizes the relationship of the three, for, born on June 8, 1878, the boy was called Burton Parker Twichell. All three ministers became closely associated with Bushnell, then retired because of ill health, and all three became, in effect, disciples of the man who had been called heretic. The logical reasonableness of his theories found sympathetic understanding in the ministers of three of Hartford's leading churches. Thus Bushnell's influence continued for many years in the city.

Horace Bushnell himself deserves to be known for more than his theories. Prominent in civic and educational matters, he took part in many activities outside his church. It was he who convinced the city authorities to make an undeveloped and then unpleasant area in central Hartford into a park, later named for him. Although in 1840 he had refused the presidency of Middlebury College, he accepted without salary for a time the presidency of the College of California while on a visit there for his health. He also selected the site for that college. He selected the route which was adopted for the Pacific Railroad.

Numerous other projects of Bushnell's would have to be considered in a complete study of the man, but their significance here is primarily their effect on his three followers in Hartford churches, for in these matters they followed his lead, also. All three were likewise active in educational and civic matters, thus, in a sense, taking part in community activities as their Puritan forebears had done, although not in the theocratic manner.

Like Bushnell, they considered all knowledge legitimate sermon material. When Twichell, like others of his time, found that scientific evolution could be adopted as not contradictory to religious beliefs, but as supplementary, he was following in the logical, rational patterns of thought which Bushnell had adopted. To Twichell, evolution meant primarily that progress was inevitable. Just as man was the physical culmination of earlier forms of life which had been directed toward the goal of his creation, so spiritually he must and would develop toward a higher and higher form.

Twichell believed that the most important part of the minister's function from the pulpit was to bring a moral lesson to his people; this idea had been impressed upon him from the beginning of his ministerial duties when he was a chaplain. Doctrine was only to serve a moral purpose, not to be an end in itself.

He turned what little knowledge he had of scientific matters to this kind of moral preaching. He had a great deal of respect for scientific methods of research and scientific caution in coming to conclusions. He said:

> The ways of science are the ways of meekness, and its triumphs are meek triumphs. It searches for knowledge on which to rest its conclusions. There is something genuinely sublime in its unwearied quest of facts. . . . And when it has found them it bows to them. That is meekness to read the facts and accept what they say. The opposite is the spirit that says: "This thing is so because I say so or some other man says so, and if the facts contradict it, so much the worse for the facts. . . ."[8]

With this respect for the techniques of science and the possible achievements which might result if scientific method were applied in all areas of human thought, Twichell frequently used scientific terminology to prove a moral point. Always optimistic, he saw man as having possibilities of great spiritual improvement, through processes of evolution. In a speech at an annual dinner of the New England Society of the City of New York, December 22, 1891, he spoke of the contributions of the forefathers of the country.

> It was their high calling to stand by the divine cause of human progress at a momentous crisis of its evolution, and they were more worthy to be put on duty at that post. Evolution! I hardly dare speak the word, knowing so little about the thing. It represents a great matter, of which I am humbly conscious of being . . . far from surrounding. . . .
> But, deficient as one's knowledge of evolution, scientifically and in detail, may be, he may have attained to a not unintelligent perception of the all-embracing creative process called by that name as that in which, in the whole range of the advancing universal movement of life, what is ascends from what was, and fulfils it.[9]

Man was always at the very center of his preaching. Through evolution, man had reached his present physical form. Through spiritual evolution, he could become better spiritually. Man's problems were capable of solution through rational, logical processes, and the individual man was all-important and capable of great things.

Christian manhood was, thus, an ever-recurring theme in his sermons and lectures. Through the spirit of Christ, and the example of Christ's life, man could overcome many obstacles. In spite of circumstances of any kind, a man could always be a man. His sermons on this subject follow a definite pattern and are divided into two main arguments. One theme is a continuation of the early Puritan idea of the soldier-Christian, struggling ever onward in spite of difficulties. Closely related to this were the examples which he took from his own war experience of strength and courage which he had witnessed in the three important years which he had spent with the 71st New York State Infantry. At Gettysburg, his heart had been with the 71st as the men he had come to know so well forged into battle. They were men without much social background; they had shocked him with their behavior and language when he first joined them in 1861; but he had come to see that in spite of the circumstances of their past lives, under the pressures of war, they were men.

This, he felt, was the most important part of Christ's teaching, the elevation of the individual man to a place where he could fulfill the promises of his being. Scientific evolution merely supplemented his theory. Certainly this physical evolution would inevitably be paralleled by spiritual development. This was completely in line with the theories of Horace Bushnell, whose influence on Burton, Parker, and Twichell affected the development of thought in their three large churches.

There is one basic difference, however, between Bushnell and Twichell; that is the fact that Twichell was never primarily a theologian. While studying in school and college, he had been perfectly satisfied to accept and remember what he was taught. Having been impressed with Bushnell when he first heard him years before in Plainville, he had wondered as an adult just what the man's doctrinal views actually were. Becoming familiar with them, he adopted them and adapted them for his own use.

This change in point of view does not indicate a lack of sincerity or conviction on his part; nor did he become more or less ardent about his ministry after he became a "Bushnellian." Like Bushnell, he was interested in freedom of thought and in rational explanations for doctrinal problems, and in Bushnell's writings he found material congenial to his own mind and experiences. Even then, however, he did not become doctrinal in his approach to his ministry. His interests continued to be primarily humanitarian. His sermons were dependent on ordinary reason rather than on doctrine. He was more concerned in having his parishioners lead Christian lives than he was in what they believed in matters strictly doctrinal.

Bushnell's significance as a theologian has never been completely evaluated. That his views were radical for his time and that portions of twentieth century liberal Protestantism have stemmed from such views seem to be evident. His work came at a strategic time, when revision was needed if Congregationalism were to survive a new time and new thought. His views on language and on theological matters were based on rational processes of thought and could be understood by thinking men at a time when men were beginning to have more and more confidence that science would provide them with logical answers to many things which had previously been mysteries.

Andrew D. White said of him:

> I have long been convinced that Bushnell is one of the greatest men that New England has ever produced. Ever since reading "Work and Play," I have felt sure that his place in the history of American literature is among the very highest. As to his position among philosophical thinkers in the United States, I should also award him a place among those of the very highest rank.[10]

A new and thorough re-evaluation of Horace Bushnell's contributions to American thought should be made. This brief summary has only touched upon his work, but it seems evident that Horace Bushnell contributed much to nineteenth and twentieth century liberal Protestantism, perhaps as much as any other one thinker of his century. His practical, rational mind pointed Christianity toward men rather than toward theory, emphasized freedom, and led not only to revisions of theological thinking, but also to improvements in educational theory.

The man alone would not have been able to accomplish all of this, however, if he had not been followed by the Burton, Parker, Twichell trio. They continued to preach his ideas after the heat of the controversy had died down. They also used his technique in applying his approach to later developments. They recognized their relation to Bushnell, and were proud of it, as is evidenced by Twichell's brief article on Bushnell's death, which he called, "A Word from Another Hartford Disciple."

All three men served their churches for many years and established Bushnell's Congregationalism as the norm for Hartford. Today this thought is still basically the foundation of, not only

Hartford, but of United States Congregationalism. The pulpit in a Hartford church, which after a merger became the descendant of Bushnell's own church, symbolizes this fact in its dedication plaque to Bushnell. The present congregation may face a different man, but they see before them the name of his predecessor, and they hear the views of a Bushnell disciple of the third, or perhaps fourth, generation. In Hartford, these theories saw their start with Bushnell, and their continuation in the trio of whom Twichell became the best known.

Thus, it took Twichell only a short time after his arrival in the city to take his place in the biggest crisis in nineteenth century Congregationalism, and to make a firm contribution to it. Not theologically so great or so important as Horace Bushnell, he was, nevertheless, very significant as a clergyman.

VI

❧

Twichell Meets Twain: The Beginning of an Important Friendship

DURING THE WINTER of 1867-1868, Mark Twain came to Hartford to oversee the publication of *Innocents Abroad*. While in the city, he stayed with his publisher Elisha Bliss, who lived at 821 Asylum Avenue, across the street from the still fairly new Asylum Hill Congregational Church. Since no steeple had yet been built on the church (nor had one grown from the good root, as Charles Dudley Warner had jokingly suggested), it was certainly a strange-looking church to Twain, who was the one to nickname it the "stub-tailed church." After he had been with Bliss for a few days and heard about Asylum Hill's parishioners and their financial standing, he re-named it the "Church of the Holy Speculators," much to his host's dismay. But to Mark Twain it seemed to represent all that he did not like about organized Christianity: Congregational, it had its roots deep in the Calvinism which he had begun to resist years before in Hannibal, Missouri; wealthy, it represented the tie between Protestantism and capitalism at which it was so easy to sneer.

Because he was anxious to be accepted in Hartford where his book was being published, Twain did not say much to anyone besides Mr. and Mrs. Bliss about this church which so amused him. Finally, however, at an evening reception in the home of one of its members to which Mrs. Bliss had taken him for the purpose of getting him acquainted with Hartford people, he could resist no longer. All might have gone well if someone else had not mentioned the church, and then Mark Twain loudly and vehemently declared it to be the "Church of the Holy Speculators." His disapproval was obvious in his voice.

To the tall, slender man behind him at the moment, the phrase came as something of a shock. He, like others, had been amused by the "stub-tailed" description which had been reported to him, but this second contribution seemed to be a little too much for him. He started to say something, then stopped as Mrs. Bliss, standing beside Mark Twain, turned around. She whispered something to Twain (which Twichell learned later was a warning that the pastor of the "slandered" church was behind him), and then introduced the two men.[1] Thus began a friendship which was eventually to include the wives and children of both men.

Soon after this first meeting, the Twichells invited Twain to their home for an evening. Twichell had become interested on first acquaintance with the personality of this stranger in the Hartford group, for Clemens came from a different kind of background from anyone whom Joe had known well. Born in Florida, Missouri, on November 30, 1835, he was the son of a family who had caught the frontier spirit and had moved restlessly from Virginia to Kentucky, hence to Missouri. When Sam was four, the family moved again, this time to Hannibal, Missouri, where he was to spend the remainder of his boyhood years. The story of his early years is well known, and obviously very different from the years that Twichell had spent in Southington, at Yale and Union, and in the Civil War.

While Twichell was thus occupied, Twain had been moving around. When his father died, the twelve-year-old boy became an apprentice printer to his brother in Hannibal, and then worked as a printer in Chicago, Philadelphia, Keokuk, and Cincinnati. In 1857 he started for New Orleans on the Mississippi River, met the pilot Horace Bixby, and was able to fulfil a boyhood dream by becoming an apprentice pilot. Under Bixby's direction, he learned the twelve hundred miles of the Mississippi River, and spent the next four years on the River.

When the outbreak of the Civil War brought about the end of much of the river traffic because of the effectiveness of Confederate blockades, Twain took part in a brief venture as soldier in the Confederate Army in a rather disorganized group of volunteers. Finding himself not much good at or much interested in soldiering, he was not at all displeased when the irregularly-formed outfit decided to break up.

Next he went to Nevada with his brother who had been appointed secretary to the governor and who needed an assistant. In 1862, he joined the staff of a Virginia City paper and adopted the pseudonym Mark Twain which he was to use thereafter. Moving from there to San Francisco, he continued in journalistic

activities, writing what was to be his first well-known story in 1865,
"The Celebrated Jumping Frog of Calaveras County."

A trip to the Sandwich Islands, about which he wrote a series
of letters, was followed by a series of lectures on the Islands,
which eventually took him east. In 1867, he toured the Mediterranean and the Holy Land, about which he wrote his second book,
The Innocents Abroad, published in 1869.

It was at this point in his career that he first visited in Hartford
to see about the publication of the *Innocents,* on which he was
then at work. His first book, *The Celebrated Jumping Frog of
Calaveras County and Other Sketches* had been published earlier,
in 1867.

To Twichell, then, here was a different sort of individual, and
his interest in people of all kinds attracted his attention to this
man immediately. Their first meeting had been very brief, and
Twichell had probably been left with the impression of a rough
but genial individual, somehow simultaneously crude and gentle,
outspoken yet friendly, almost on the defensive, yet giving the
perceptive clergyman the idea that he really wanted to make
friends.

One evening at the Twichells' home, and Mark Twain had
completely cemented a relationship that would continue. With
only Joe, Harmony, and the few-month-old Edward Carrington
Twichell, Twain found it easy to relax. The two men found quickly
that they were much alike in their wit and humorous reactions to
various situations. Harmony was pleased with the somewhat
awkward yet courtly grace with which Twain always attempted
to treat women. Twain, always fond of babies, held the young
Edward with great care, fearing that he might break, and easily
charmed the hearts of the young parents. That first evening at
the Twichells' was the most relaxed that Mark had spent thus
far in Hartford, where previously he had been happy and well
treated, but had felt slightly awkward and out of place.

On his next trip to Hartford, shortly thereafter, Twain stayed
with the Twichells and got to know them all much better. He
and Joe took the first of their many long walks together, hiking
out to Talcott Mountain and back, talking and laughing much
of the time. That Twichell was a minister did not seem to affect
Twain one way or another. Since it would be months before they
would settle down to discuss theological and philosophical matters,
they had these early occasions for non-controversial matters only.

At this time in Twichell's life it was, perhaps, good for the friendship that Clemens had been a Confederate volunteer for only a very short time, because it would be some time before Twichell could accept old enemies as friends. Twain may not, of course, even have mentioned it this early in their acquaintance; but since Twichell's own Civil War experiences were so numerous and fresh in his mind, it seems likely that the subject did arise. Knowing battle situations himself, Twichell could probably only be amused at Mark's one adventure, and gave him, perhaps, more credit than he deserved for withdrawing from an infamous cause.

These early visits were important in several ways for both men. To Twichell, they were most refreshing breaks in the struggle of establishing a new church. It was a decided pleasure to get away from these problems for a while, and also to be treated as a man, not as a clergyman, at this time before he had had much chance for developing close personal friendships among his parishioners. He must have found great delight in having someone to talk with who was as amused as he inwardly was at the accoustical and structural problems of the Gothic beauty that had been constructed on Asylum Avenue. It was also good to talk about other things, and to listen to a really good story-teller tell tales of the western frontier, the Sandwich Islands, and the Mediterranean region. The break from the active life of the army camp to the serious problems of a city parish could not have been easy for a young man who, no matter how seriously he might take his ministry, could not help but feel oppressed occasionally by heavy responsibilities, so different from anything he had previously experienced.

For Twain, this was his first *in*formal friendship in the East. He had plodded, perhaps somewhat awkwardly, from formal party to formal reception with the Blisses, and had talked of business matters with his publishers. He, too, was still young, desirous of physical activity and really jovial companionship, and, even more than the Connecticut-born Twichell, was probably oppressed by the surface formality of most of his Hartford relationships. Later, he would have many friends and would feel very much at home in Hartford, but certainly at first he did not feel completely comfortable except with Joe alone and in the Twichell home.

Harmony had sensed the inner struggle that Joe was experiencing in adjusting to his new life and had worried a little about the rapidity with which he had assumed the responsibilities of becoming, within a few years, a minister, a husband, and then a father. She had realized that all of this was a comparatively sudden change for a man whose previous life had included only study and the three-year period as Civil War chaplain. It was not diffi- cult for her to recognize the good that his friendship with Clemens was doing for him, and she was only too happy to welcome his newly-made friend to their home. He surprised her on occasion, at first, with his humor and frankness, but she was not easily startled, and her own sense of humor responded to his.

About this early stage of their friendship, Twichell wrote:

> I first met him in the winter of 1867-8 when—lately come from California,—he was in Hartford overseeing the publication of "The Innocents Abroad," from the issue of which dates his emer- gence into universal public notice and favor as an author. Of the shining, world-wide fame he was destined to attain, no one then dreamed—himself least of all. We were both young men, and the acquaintance so begun grew into a friendship which continued unbroken even after that, and went on strengthening with the flight of years. I cannot say that at that period we were wholly sympathetic in either thought or feeling. Our antecedent condi- tions and experience in life had been very different, and, in some ways, contrasted. But while originally attracted to him by the brightness of his mind, the incomparable charm of his talk, and his rare companionableness, I was not long in finding out that he had a big, warm and tender heart. He bore, indeed, marks of the rude society of the frontier and the mining-camp in which his youth was passed. He was eminently a man "with the bark on." He was composed of elements strangely mixed,—in this and that respect to appearance contradictory. Exterior roughnesses he had; also, underneath them, exquisite refinements of taste and senti- ment.[2]

While the above was written many years later, after Mark Twain had died, it seems to be, nevertheless, a fair statement of Twichell's original reactions. Here was no "lion-hunting," as has been claimed by some of the critics of Mark Twain, for it was several years after their first meeting that Twain began to receive general acclaim, and some years after that before he gained na- tional and international reputation. At the time of this first meet- ing, as Twichell pointed out, Twain was still a man "with the bark on," and his future fame had nothing to do with the be- ginnings of the friendship.

To Twain, the fine spirit in the Twichell home was impressive. Even in small matters, Harmony pleased him, for while he had found some Hartford homes where smoking in the parlor was frowned upon, Harmony did not even seem to be aware of the blue haze with which he and Joe could impregnate the house in the long, winter evenings.

During one of these long evenings, in a fairly mellow mood after an afternoon hike, a brief time with young Edward before he went to bed, and a good meal, Mark and Joe settled down for a smoke. As soon as the dishes were done, Harmony brought in some sewing and joined them. Soon Twain put into words a feeling he had had for some time about the harmonious relationship of the Twichell home, and expressed his own envy of their happiness as a family. He was then thirty-four, fairly prosperous as a result of lectures, and *Innocents Abroad* was due to be published shortly, which his publisher insisted would establish his reputation as one of America's first-rate writers.

Close as they had become, the Twichells had never realized that a sense of loneliness enveloped Mark Twain. Even at this time, their conversations had rarely been personal in a soul-searching sense. That he should envy their happiness seemed a tragedy to the Twichells. Mrs. Twichell asked him why he did not marry and establish a home of his own.

Twain replied that he was in love and described the girl to them, but said that he was afraid she would not marry him. His sensitivity and feelings of inferiority made him even feel that she ought not to accept him. When he said that he had not dared to ask her, Joe and Harmony both insisted that he should propose. Having seen beneath the rough exterior themselves, they felt sure that a woman such as he had described would see, too, the fine characteristics which had appealed to them. They assured him over and over that she would undoubtedly accept his proposal.

On February 2, 1870,, Mr. and Mrs. Twichell went from Hartford to Elmira, New York, where Twichell and the Rev. Thomas K. Beecher, pastor of the Park Congregational Church in Elmira, performed the wedding ceremony for Samuel Clemens and Olivia Langdon.

At this time the Twichells added another friend to the growing circle. Thomas Beecher, brother of Henry Ward Beecher, spent most of his life in Elmira as pastor of the Congregational church there. After this first meeting, he and Twichell visited each other occasionally, and, conveniently for both, traded pulpits in later years when Joe wanted to be in Elmira with Mark, and Thomas K. wanted to be in Hartford.

Charmed quickly by the Twichells, Twain's bride was a welcome addition to the friendly group. Before long the two families would be living within a few blocks of each other in Hartford, and dashing back and forth between the houses frequently. It would not be long before small Clemenses and small Twichells would have, for their favorite "adopted" relatives, Uncle Joe, Aunt Harmony, Uncle Mark, and Aunt Livy. But first there was a brief period of residence in Buffalo, New York, for the Clemenses.

It is never completely possible to understand all that goes into the making of a friendship between two people, because they may be alike or different, close in age, or far apart, etc., and outsiders may never understand why they become friends. Twichell and Twain, very different in backgrounds and beliefs, found something in each other which each quickly liked. That Twain could overlook the parts of Twichell's theology with which he might disagree does not seem improbable, because Joe was a good companion, active, athletic, often gay. That Twichell could accept Twain with his roughnesses, as well as his unorthodox beliefs, is only slightly more difficult to understand.

Much of Twichell's background would indicate that he should have disapproved highly of a man like Twain. Coming from a small Connecticut town, immersed in a still not-very-liberal Congregationalism, Twichell could easily have objected so strenuously to Twain's beliefs that friendship would have been impossible, because tolerance had never been a Puritan virtue. Likewise, his father's position in a small town, his own education at Yale, Union, and Andover, had led Twichell into a social pattern where one did not exhibit differences from the norm.

Without Twichell's Civil War experiences, it seems safe to say that he and Mark Twain could never have "hit it off" so quickly and so well. During the War, however, in the rough and tough 71st New York State Infantry, Twichell had become used to many things previously out of his ken. He had come to recognize much good concealed under rough exteriors in these men with whom he had lived so closely. He had heard and seen much in those years. Even such a matter as profanity had come to seem to him not so horrible as he had previously felt. Rough, uncultured, even unintelligent speech he had become accustomed to; and, in comparison, Twain's roughness was a mild affair, mixed as it was with geniality, wit, and keen intelligence.

More important to Twichell himself, however, as preparation for this relationship with Twain, had been his friendship with

Father O'Hagan. Forced to spend much time together by the circumstances of war, they had found in each other much in common in their mutual sympathy with mankind, in their earnest desire to serve their regiment, and in their personalities, so that they had come to enjoy each other's company very much. O'Hagan, the Jesuit, the extreme of the conservatives, had proved to be a man whom Twichell could accept, admire, and sincerely like. Their backgrounds had been different, too.

Now, Twichell was really confronted with a very similar situation. Here was another man with a background very different from his own. If from Twichell's mid-nineteenth century Congregational point of view, O'Hagan had seemed to be extremely conservative theologically, so Mark Twain, from the same point of view, would appear extremely liberal. Since O'Hagan and Twichell had been friends, why not Twain and Twichell? Twichell probably never worked out that particular train of thought consciously, but the facts indicate that there was such a progression.

That such a development occurred in Twichell's broadening is further evidenced by his desire to have his two friends get together. He was, apparently, sure that he had found, at two religious extremes, two men very much the same at heart, and he had to get them together. In this attempt he succeeded, and O'Hagan and Twain soon became friends. On February 1, 1875, Twain wrote to C. W. Stoddard that he was going to Worcester, Massachusetts, with Joe,

> . . . to have a "time" with a most jolly and delightful Jesuit priest who was all through the war with Joe. . . . I sent the Padre word that I knew all about the Jesuits, from the Sunday-school books and that I was well aware that he wanted to get Joe and me into his den and skin us and make religious parchment out of us after the ancient style of his communion since the days of good Loyola, but that I was willing to chance it and trust to Providence.[3]

That no records of the conversations of these three are available is too bad; they must have been lively.

Mark Twain seems to have wanted to live in Hartford shortly after his first visits to that city. As early as June, 1869, before his marriage, Twain attempted to buy a part interest in the Hartford *Courant,* but was turned down as a complete unknown by Charles Dudley Warner and Joseph Hawley. If he had waited a few months, until *Innocents Abroad* was firmly established as a success, his response from the conservative *Courant* men might have been different; but, by the time that Twain's position was established, it was too late for them to change their minds.

It is interesting to note that Twain, apparently, never held this early decision of theirs against them, but became friendly later with both men, particularly Warner, with whom he collaborated in the writing of *The Gilded Age.* It seems possible, at least, to assume that he was willing, in this one instance at any rate, to accept these men for what they were.

When his father-in-law, Jervis Langdon, bought him a one-third interest in the Buffalo *Express,* Twain had to give up his desire to live in Hartford, at least for a while. Although he liked Buffalo and many of the people there, and was well accepted from the beginning of his contacts in the city, Twain was not happy. He and Livy, apparently, made no close friends, except the David Grays. It was a somewhat lonely time for both of them, newly married, newly moved, unacquainted with the community, and for some reason, unable to find their place in it. Nor did the paper prosper.

Then a series of greater tragedies struck. Jervis Langdon died. A friend of Livy's died unexpectedly in their home. Mark's and Livy's first child was born prematurely, and for some time both mother and child were not well.

In 1871, during the summer, Twain again visited Hartford on business, this time to deliver the manuscript of *Roughing It* to his publishers. They were excited about the unexpectedly great success of *Innocents Abroad,* which had surpassed even their high hopes for it, and were waiting anxiously to get another book by Twain in print before the enthusiasm aroused by the *Innocents* died down. Again, Twain found that he felt about Hartford and its people as he had at first, that this was a place where he could be happy, where he and Livy could make more of a home than they had succeeded in doing in Buffalo. An evening with the Twichells, Joe, Harmony, Edward, and now Julia Curtis Twichell (born 1869), further convinced Twain that here was where he wanted to establish his own family.

Because he had to sell the house in Buffalo, which had been a wedding present from Livy's father, before he could build in Hartford, he looked for a place to rent. He discovered, finally, that the Hookers would rent their house to him. On October 1, 1871, the Clemens family arrived in Hartford.

VII

❧

Twichell and Twain: Personal Aspects of the Friendship

AFTER THE CLEMENS family moved to Hartford, the two men seem to have found that their early liking for each other could develop into a lasting friendship. While their families were to become well acquainted and to visit back and forth at each other's homes, there was always a very close personal relationship between the two men in which their families did not entirely share. They found, apparently, in this companionship, relaxation and pleasure which took them away temporarily from their mature responsibilities, for a spirit of boyish enthusiasm permeated this friendship through the years. Often boys at heart, they found in each other this delightful similarity which could be a shared experience.

A personal friendship, however, between two such men as Twain and Twichell, literary figure and minister, could not be a completely separate thing from their professional lives. It was inevitable that each would influence the other in many ways. Most important was Twichell's influence on Mark Twain's literary production; for, without this factor, the friendship between the two would have little significance today. It thus becomes necessary to look for the effect of Twichell on Twain's writing, and to determine its nature and value.

Conclusions have been drawn in much Twain scholarship that Twichell influenced Twain's writing harmfully by trying to cast him into a mold of respectability in Connecticut Congregational terms, and that this resulted in repressions of Twain's spontaneous literary productions. Some critics have felt that the combination of Livy and Joe was more than the most creative of artists could overcome, and that the addition of Hartford society, including men like Warner and the frequent visitor William Dean Howells, made it a wonder that Twain was able to write anything at all. This is a facile observation, because it is difficult to picture a man

of Twain's temperament at home in the Hartford and Asylum
Hill Church circles into which he found himself precipitated thus
early in his writing career.

That the Clemens family were happy there, Howells himself
recognized. On one occasion, after he and Thomas Bailey Aldrich
had spent several days in Hartford visiting the Clemens and
Warner families and meeting their friends, Howells wrote:

> In the good-fellowship of that cordial neighborhood we had two
> such days as the aging sun no longer shines on in his round. There
> was constant running in and out of friendly houses where the
> lively hosts and guests called one another by their Christian names
> or nicknames, and no such vain ceremony as knocking or ringing
> at doors.[1]

Much is omitted in any kind of surface generalization which
would indicate that Twichell's effect on Mark Twain the writer
was to repress or to restrict his freedom of expression, either in
subject matter or in language. By the end of the Civil War, as
has been seen, Twichell himself was far from being the narrow
clergyman who before the war had worried about the possibility
of association with an Episcopalian. Yet, unfortunately, it is this
kind of clergyman who has often been described in the studies of
Twain's life and writing when Twichell has been mentioned.

Before an objective analysis of the beneficial or detrimental effect of the Twichell influence on Twain can be made, it is necessary to examine the nature of the relationship between the two
men. Just how close was their friendship? What did they actually
do together? What did they talk about? What did they write to
and about each other?

For convenience, the relationship can be broken down into
three phases: first, the personal relationship between the men and
their families, irrespective of their professional lives; second, the
religious relationship, including their agreements and disagreements, and the actual participation, or lack of it, of Twain in
Twichell's church and professional life; third, the important matter of literary influence—which can only be understood when the
personal and religious aspects are first determined.

The personal side of the friendship includes the relationship
between the two men, between their families, and their participation in community affairs together. First of all, they did many
things together. One of their frequent activities, for example, was
the long hike up Talcott Mountain, five miles away. When Twi-

chell's parish responsibilities and Twain's writing schedule per-
mitted it, they started out on this familiar trek.

People who remembered seeing them going along have reported
that they talked all the way, waving their arms, and often talking
both at once. These conversations seem to have been, generally,
of a light nature, not involving serious thought or decisions. They
filled in for each other the history of their past lives before they
met, Mississippi River boat days from Mark Twain, Civil War
experiences from Twichell, as well as other things.

Some of their experiences together were of a more ridiculous
nature than the Talcott Mountain hikes, particularly an attempted hike to Boston, Massachusetts, 110 miles from Hartford.
After several years of short-distance hiking around the city, they
decided that a real expedition on foot was next in order. Accordingly, after laying careful plans, on November 12, 1874, they
started for Boston—on foot.

Leaving at 8:30 in the morning, they took a carriage for the
first few miles, down Farmington Avenue, through the business
center of Hartford, as far as the bridge across the Connecticut
River to East Hartford. Then they took to the road, Twain carrying the basket of lunch, Twichell a small bag of personal possessions. The first day they got as far as a tavern in Westford, a
tavern with, as Twichell said, "a sublimely profane hostler whom
you couldn't jostle with any sort of mild remark without bringing
down upon yourself a perfect avalanche of oaths."[2]

At the end of this first day, they were both tired, and Twain's
feet were not performing as well as he had hoped. They enjoyed
the tavern with its entertaining hostler, however, and after a
night's sleep continued their walking.

Six miles on foot the second day was all they found they wanted,
so at North Ashford they took a train for Boston, after wiring
Howells and Redpath that they were on their way to Young's Hotel.

Howells replied immediately, wiring to the hotel: "You and
Twichell come right up to 37 Concord Avenue, Cambridge, near
observatory. Party waiting for you." At about nine that evening
they arrived in Cambridge.

Not willing to admit defeat, the two hikers insisted that they
had planned to finish the trip by train, and then entertained the
group with accounts of their expedition.

Howells said of this evening:

I can see him [Twain] now as he stood up in the midst of our
friends with his head thrown back, and in his hand a dish of

those escalloped oysters without which no party in Cambridge was
really a party, exulting in the tale of his adventures, which had
abounded in the most original characters and amusing incidents
at every mile of their progress.[3]

When the newspapers in Boston and Hartford picked the story
up and printed it, complete with illustrations, Twichell was
slightly abashed, wondering how his parishioners would react to
such nonsense, because this was the first time that he and Twain
had become involved together in a ridiculous adventure amusing
enough for the newspapers to cover in detail. His church people,
however, were as amused as the rest of the citizens of Boston and
Hartford and joined in the general merriment over the escapade.
Twichell had then been their pastor for seven years, and they
knew and liked him well enough to realize that this kind of adventure did not indicate any real lack of ministerial sincerity or
dignity. There is at least suspicion, also, that as good business men
they minded not at all some good free publicity.

Besides these occasional hikes, there were many evenings spent
at each other's homes. Often these were just quiet times for the
two men. Often, too, they were opportunities for each man to become acquainted with the friends of the other. Aldrich, Howells,
and other literary figures were often at Twain's; and Twichell
became a real part of the literary group there gathered.

Visiting celebrities he met also, including Matthew Arnold,
who as late as 1883 had still not accepted Mark Twain as an
important writer. When in Boston, he stopped to see Howells,
and, being told that Howells was in Hartford with Twain, Arnold
said to Mrs. Howells, "Oh, but he doesn't like *that* sort of thing,
does he?"

Mrs. Howells replied, "He likes Mr. Clemens very much, and
he thinks him one of the greatest men he ever knew."[4]

It was only a short time later that Arnold lectured in Hartford,
met Mark Twain, and dined at his home with the Twichells and
the Rev. Dr. Edwin Pond Parker. Like so many others, personal
acquaintance was all that was necessary, and Arnold found that
he agreed with Howells, Twichell, Parker, and the many others
who had come to recognize and appreciate the character and personality of the man Clemens.

At the same time, Twain was, perhaps inevitably, becoming an
adopted member of the Yale '59 group, who continued their college friendships and found Twichell's a convenient meeting place.

Half way between Boston and New York on the New York, New Haven, and Hartford Railroad, Hartford made a central location for many groups. One of the most frequent guests at Twichell's was the only available one of the other three Yale '59ers who had gone on together to New York after graduating from Yale. Carrington had been killed; Stiles had remained in the South; but T. R. Lounsbury, now a professor at Yale, continued as one of Joe's closest personal friends.

The complete freedom from formal restraint of this aspect of the friendship was, perhaps, best expressed by Mark Twain. Writing to Howells to urge him to come to Hartford for a visit, Twain said:

> You will find us the most reasonable people in the world. We had thought of precipitating upon you, George Warner and his wife one day, Twichell and his jewel of a wife another day, and Charles Perkins and wife another. Only those—simply members of our family they are. But I'll close the door against them all, which will "fix" all of the lot except Twichell, who will no more hesitate to climb in the back window than *nothing*.[5]

Having had their hikes and other kinds of social companionship in Hartford for several years, Twain and Twichell soon began to feel that a longer trip would be enjoyable together, and in 1877 they took the first of several such jaunts. On May 16, 1877, they started for Bermuda, where, under assumed names, they stayed at a Mrs. Kirkham's boarding house.

The trip was a considerable success, and for the first time of many, Twichell could not resist revealing Mark Twain's identity to the other boarders at Mrs. Kirkham's. He waited until he and Twain were just ready to leave, and then dashed back to tell the others who Twain was. They both promised to return the next year, and, perhaps, to make a yearly visit; but it was exactly thirty years later, in 1907, before they did return together.

One of the longest and most important trips which they took together was the walking tour in Europe in 1878, about which Twain wrote his *A Tramp Abroad*.

Twain had gone to Europe to gather material for a book. Twichell had been unable to accompany him because of church and family responsibilities—there were, by now, five young Twichells. Joe was also hard pressed for money, as he was most of his life because of his immoderate generosity, even though his church paid him comparatively well.

On June 8, 1878, however, he received a letter from Twain inviting him to join him as his guest during the summer. His sixth child had been born that morning—Burton Parker Twichell, named for the friendly trio of Hartford Congregational ministers. He wrote to Twain:

> I am almost too joyful for pleasure. I labor with my felicities. How I shall get to sleep tonight I don't know, though I have had a good start, in not having slept much last night. Oh, my! *do* you realize, Mark, what a symposium it is to be? I do. To begin with, I am thoroughly tired and the rest will be worth everything. To walk with you and talk with you for weeks together—why, it's my dream of luxury. Harmony, who at sunrise this morning deemed herself the happiest woman on the Continent when I read your letter to her, widened her smile perceptively, and revived another degree of strength in a minute. She refused to consider her being left alone, but only the great chance opened to me.
>
> SHOES—Mark, remember that ever so much of our pleasure depends upon your shoes. Don't fail to have adequate preparation made in that department.[6]

From the beginning to the end, the trip was enjoyable for Twichell. His pleasure began on the trip over. He sailed at the end of July with Edwin Pond Parker, who was also Europe-bound. Since in Twichell's lifetime, Yale '59 men appeared at all times in all places, much to the amusement of his Hartford friends, he, of course, met one on shipboard. Many other friends and acquaintances were also on the ship—General Terry's sister, a Miss Brinley of Hartford, and Miss Cowley, a friend of hers.

In London, Parker and Twichell spent two days doing some sightseeing together and spent an evening with General Hawley and Will Hammersley. Clutching a newly-acquired tall hat and sporting a newly-grown mustache, Joe left London for Strasbourg.

On August 2, 1878, Twichell joined the Clemens family at Baden Baden. From there, the two men tramped through the Black Forest, walking most of the time, with the Clemens family following occasionally by train.

As was his custom on this sort of tramp, Mark Twain enjoyed not being known, while Twichell still found pleasure in revealing Twain's identity just as they were leaving various groups of people whom they met along the way.

It was on this trip that Twichell put into writing, more than he did at any other time, his reactions to Mark Twain's personality. His letters home were filled with anecdotes of their journey, along with his feelings about Twain. Some of these are interesting to compare with Twain's telling of the incidents in *A Tramp Abroad*. About one episode, Twain said:

> I needed exercise, so I employed my agent [Harris, who is Twichell] in setting stranded logs and dead trees adrift, and I sat on a boulder and watched them go whirling and leaping head over heels down the boiling torrent. When I had had exercise enough, I made the agent take some, by running a race with one of those logs. I made a trifle by betting on the log.[7]

Twichell's report varies from this one; it is, probably, the true version, because it was written not for publication, but as news for his family at home. According to Twichell:

> Mark is a queer fellow. There is nothing that he so delights in as a swift, strong stream. You can hardly get him to leave one when once he is within the influence of its fascinations. To throw stones and sticks seems to afford him rapture. To-night, as we were on our way back to the hotel, seeing a lot of driftwood caught by the torrent side below the path, I climbed down and threw it in. When I got back to the path Mark was running down-stream after it as hard as he could go, throwing up his hands and shouting in the wildest ecstasy, and when a piece went over a fall and emerged into view in the foam below he would jump up and down and yell. He said afterward that he hadn't been so excited in three months. He acted just like a boy; another feature of his extreme sensitiveness in certain directions. . . .[8]

On this extended trip together, each man had more opportunity than had ever occurred before to observe the other in varying circumstances, and, thus, to come to an even greater understanding of each other. Twichell had long noted the obvious occasional roughnesses in Twain, along with his thoughtfulness and gentleness and had been unable to reconcile completely these diverse aspects of Twain's make-up. Harmony had also been aware of the often contradictory nature of the man and, more than her husband, had wished that Mark's behavior could be depended upon. She was often just a little afraid that Joe might somehow be hurt by Twain's actions. Knowing how much the friendship meant to him, she hoped that nothing would spoil it.

Often the Twichells had discussed their friend, and Joe always hoped that nothing would happen to upset Harmony enough to create any lasting awkwardness in the families' friendly relations. Often he was the one who attempted to "cover" for his friend, to explain away the crudities in terms of Mark's early years of frontier living and comparative newness in eastern society. Again on this trip, with his own understanding growing, he tried to help Harmony see Mark as he saw him. In a letter home, he said:

> He has coarse spots in him. But I never knew a person so finely regardful of the feelings of others in some ways. He hates to pass another person walking, and will practise some subterfuge to take off what he feels is the discourtesy of it. And he is exceedingly timid, tremblingly timid, about approaching strangers; hates to ask a question. His sensitive regard for others extends to animals. When we are driving his concern is all about the horse. He can't bear to see the whip used, or to see a horse pull hard. To-day when the driver clucked up the horse and quickened his pace a little, Mark said, "The fellow's got the notion that we are in a hurry." He is exceedingly considerate toward me in regard to everything—or most things.[9]

Twichell never, apparently, elaborated any more fully than he did here as to what he meant by the "coarse spots." It must be remembered that this was a report to his family, who also knew Twain, and who would, therefore, understand what Twichell meant from personal experience and past conversations, and who would recognize in what spirit the remark was made. Joe may even have been reassuring them that he was not blind to Twain's so-called "coarse spots" any more than they were, but he saw so many more important and fine qualities in Clemens' personality that he could overlook the shortcomings. That the friendship continued unabated would indicate that whatever these weaknesses were, they did not disturb Twichell seriously, and also that he did not make Twain feel guilty or self-conscious about them.

Twichell continued writing his long letters to his family, reports which give one of the best possible pictures of the relationship between the two men, as well as giving Twichell's analysis of Twain. When considering the nature of the two men and their relationship, these letters become much more important than *A Tramp Abroad*. In the book it is often impossible to separate the real from the imaginary. Twain wrote to Twichell after the book had been published, "You'll find reminders of things, all along, that happened to us, and of others that didn't happen; but you'll remember the spot where they were invented."[10]

After a day on Gemmi Pass, Twichell wrote, telling of the time they had spent in gathering flowers. Twain became interested in the many varieties growing there and wanted to collect some.

After Mark had filled his notebook with samples, Twichell took a stiff paper advertisement which he happened to have with him and made a cornucopia-like bag, which Twain then attached to his vest as a container for more flowers. When they returned to their hotel, Mark put the flowers in a cardboard box and mailed them to Livy.

After telling about this and a few other things which they had done, he continued:

> . . . Mark is splendid to walk with amid such grand scenery, for he talks so well about it, has such a power of strong, picturesque expression. I wish you might have heard him to-day. His vigorous speech nearly did justice to the things we saw.[11]

The six weeks that they spent together roaming through Europe on foot seems to have cemented their relationship completely. Short hikes and brief trips had been enjoyable and profitable, but this period in Europe gave them much more time to understand each other than anything else during the first eleven years of their friendship.

Later, Twichell remembered best the little incidents which intensified his appreciation of Mark's real nature, his spontaneous and natural reactions to things that had happened, uninhibited by the presence of others. For example, Twichell told in a speech many years later an incident which occurred when they were climbing the Gorner Grat.

> As we paused for a rest, a lamb from a flock of sheep near by ventured inquisitively toward us, whereupon Mark seated himself on a rock, and with beckoning hand and soft words tried to get it to come to him.
>
> On the lamb's part it was a struggle between curiosity and timidity, but in a succession of advances and retreats it gained confidence, though at a very gradual rate. It was a scene for a painter; the great American humorist on one side of the game and that silly little creature on the other, with the Matterhorn for a background. Mark was reminded that the time he was consuming was valuable—but to no purpose. The Gorner Grat could wait. He held on with undiscouraged perseverance till he carried his point; the lamb finally put its nose in his hand, and he was happy over it all the rest of the day.[12]

On September 9, 1878, Twichell said good-bye to the Clemens family at Lausanne, and left for Paris, London, and Hartford. On the next day Twain wrote to him:

DEAR OLD JOE,—It is actually all over! I was so low-spirited
at the station yesterday, and this morning, when I woke, I couldn't
seem to accept the dismal truth that you were really gone, and the
pleasant tramping and talking at an end. Ah, my boy! it has been
such a rich holiday to me, and I feel under such deep and honest
obligations to you for coming. I am putting out of my mind all
memory of the times when I misbehaved toward you and hurt you;
I am resolved to store up and remember only the charming hours
of the journeys and the times when I was not unworthy to
be with you, and share a companionship which to me stands first
after Livy's. . . .

Livy can't accept or endure the fact that you are gone. But
you *are,* and we cannot get around it. So take our love with you,
and bear it also over the sea to Harmony, and God bless you both.

MARK[13]

The "companionship which to me stands first after Livy's" was
to continue unabated throughout the remaining years of their
lives. If Twichell were aware of "coarse spots," if Clemens were
sometimes aware that he had not behaved as he would have liked
to—neither, apparently, ever made the other feel any awkwardness
about anything that had happened or had been said, for the evidence points to a continuing pleasant relationship.

When Twain no longer lived in Hartford, he continued to
visit at Twichell's and to stay there when he was in Hartford on
business. The correspondence between the two men was also full
in the later years, Mark Twain sometimes writing personal letters
containing news, sometimes entertaining Joe with long epistles
on such subjects as how to strop a razor. Joe wrote letters with
personal news from his family and their friends in Hartford as
well as letters of consolation when tragedies began to strike in the
Clemens family.

When Mark Twain has Harris (Twichell) say in *A Tramp
Abroad,* "Your Harris will never desert you. We will die together,"[14] he was only stating lightly the very close relationship
which really existed between the two men.

While the men themselves were enjoying their friendship, their
wives and children enjoyed each other's company, also. Katy
Leary, a long-time servant of the Clemens family, gives a first-hand
account of times when the two families were together:

. . . Oh, what Christmases and Thanksgivings we had! Thanks-
giving was most as wonderful as Christmas. Mrs. Clemens always

had all the people to a great dinner that day—people that wasn't very well off, poor people—not her own friends specially. Then in the evening the Warners would have a great dinner (and the Twitchells [*sic*] used to go over to the Warners for that). Then on their way back Mr. Twitchell and his wife and the nine little Twitchells used to stop at our house and then we used to play charades. The dining table was always loaded with all the candy there was—about ten dishes of candy—set all around the table near the edge, just where the little Twitchells could reach up their hands to get it and there was the little Twitchells' hands going around that table as fast as they could go until all the candy was gone. They'd empty all them dishes in no time! There was nine in the family, and no wonder![15]

Several summers, along with other Hartford people of their acquaintance, they went to the Adirondacks. Keene Valley became a second home to all of them. So impressed were they with their happy summers there that in later years two of Twichell's sons made their permanent homes at Saranac Lake. During the summers in the 1870's and 1880's, when they were all able to make the trips, the little group enjoyed themselves to the full. Hiking, some fishing, and other activities gave them all a needed break from their Hartford routines, along with the family friendships that they all enjoyed.

The youngsters liked particularly the evenings around a campfire when Twichell could usually be counted on to tell story after story for the entertainment of all, but especially the young. Always a dramatic and effective speaker, he could make the stories seem better than any stories had ever been at home, there in the mountains around the campfire. One of his specialties which the children clamored for over and over again was Uncle Remus tales.[16]

He also told them again and again of John Brown, who, he pointed out to them, had come from that part of the country and who, too, had enjoyed the very places which they were enjoying. He considered Brown one of the greatest of men.

Gradually, thus, the friendship which had started between the two men had come to include not only their immediate families, but also the Nook Farm Hartford group. There were social affairs in Hartford in which they all participated, as well as the vacations together.

Just as the Twichell children enjoyed the Clemens family (and the dishes of candy), so the young Clemenses were fond of the

Twichells. When Mark Twain's friend Theodore Crane in Elmira was ill, Twain wrote in one of his letters intended to cheer him up:

> ... You know how absent-minded Twichell is, and how desolate his face is when he is in that frame. At such times, he passes the word with a friend on the street and is not aware of the meeting at all. Twice in a week, our Clara had this latter experience with him within the past month. But the second instance was too much for her, and she woke him up, in his tracks, with a reproach. She said:—
> "Uncle Joe, *why* do you always look as if you were just going down into the grave, when you meet a person on the street?"—and then went on to reveal to him the funereal spectacle which he presented on such occasions. Well, she has met Twichell three times since then, and would swim the Connecticut to avoid meeting him the fourth. As soon as he sights her, no matter how public the place nor how far off she is, he makes a bound into the air, heaves arms and legs into all sorts of frantic gestures of delight, and so comes prancing, skipping, and pirouetting for her like a drunken Indian entering heaven.[17]

Along with the friendship between the two men themselves and the close relationship between their families, there was the participation of Twichell and Twain together in various Hartford activities. In the city, as they went together into community affairs, each man brought to the other a widening circle of acquaintances.

One of the most significant of these activities was the Monday Evening Club. In the 1860's this intellectual society had been founded by Horace Bushnell, Calvin Stowe, and J. Hammond Trumbull. Its membership was kept to twenty members who met every two weeks from October through May to hear a short paper by the member whose turn it was to perform, or by a visiting celebrity. After the reading of the essay, discussion followed, limited to ten minutes to a member. Refreshments followed, sometimes a supper, or beer and liquors (except at Twichell's).

Soon after their arrival in their Hartford pastorates, Nathaniel J. Burton, Edwin Pond Parker, and Twichell were invited to join. Other members at the time included Charles Dudley Warner, editor of the *Courant,* and rapidly becoming known as a writer of humorous essays; General Hawley; the Rev. Francis Goodwin, an Episcopal rector who lived on Woodland Street near Twichell, and who was a man of considerable wealth, cousin of J. P. Morgan; William Hammersley, a lawyer and judge, who later was involved with Twain in the disastrous Paige type-setting machine venture; Governor Henry C. Robinson; General William B. Franklin, and other prominent men in the city. Just as Twain had made it possible for Twichell to meet many of the literary figures of the day, so Twichell could help Mark Twain to become better acquainted with the intellectual leaders of the city itself.

The activities of the club indicate Mark Twain's acceptance by the group. He had been discussed by them in a panel on American humor, led by Trumbull, as early as 1865, some years before his first visit to Hartford. While the members of the group very often in later years disagreed with Twain, when he attacked the Republican Party, argued for woman suffrage, or read parts of the early versions of *What Is Man?*, they nevertheless approved of the man himself. There was never any strain in their relationship. Their arguments and discussions were for intellectual stimulation only, and the others did not find Twain's thoughts particularly shocking, even when in decided opposition to their own views.

Twain himself enjoyed the activities of the club for many years, and he often urged out-of-town literary men to come to its meetings. Howells, for example, became a fairly frequent guest.

There were other local activities in which the two men, Twain and Twichell, participated together. Some were in connection with the Asylum Hill Congregational Church and will be discussed later. One interesting situation was that of the Chinese students in Hartford. In the early 1870's the Chinese Educational Commission of the Chinese government sent a group of Chinese students to Hartford and other New England towns. The boys were to attend the public schools and then go on to college, many of them to Yale University. Yung Wing, a Yale graduate, was the Chinese official in charge of the group, and he established residence in Hartford. He attended Twichell's church and became a friend of the whole family.

His relationship with Twichell became very close, and in 1874 the two of them went to Peru where Yung Wing had been ordered by his government to look into the living conditions of the Chinese coolies. Dr. E. W. Kellogg, later to become Yung Wing's brother-in-law, also went along. The situation of the coolies was found to be very bad, and all three men were very much disturbed by what they saw. Twichell reported later:

. . . By what he [Yung Wing] heard and saw he was soon
filled with burning indignation. One day in the city of Lima,
as he was expressing his wrath more openly and freely than,
under the circumstances, consisted with prudence, he was remon-
strated with, and told that he was putting his life in peril to
talk so. Whereupon he hotly replied: "Well, suppose I am! Why
shouldn't a man put his life in peril? May be it would be the
best use I could make of my life to lay it down right here in
Lima! If I thought so, I would do it! *I should have no delicacy
about it at all!"* He was assured that, however it might be with
him, his companions *did* feel considerable delicacy upon the
subject, and wanted more time to consider it.[18]

When Twichell became interested in a subject, or project,
such as this Chinese situation, he brought his friends into it,
too. And this situation was one which disturbed him greatly.
He gave many talks all over Connecticut about Peru, lecturing
not only before large groups in the cities, but going to the
smaller places like Southington and Higganum. His friends in
Hartford heard a great deal about Peru and watched in amaze-
ment, and some amusement, as Joe went roaring around the state,
usually without pay, giving his talks.

Mark Twain, along with many others, of course, heard perhaps more than he really cared to about Peru, the problems of
the Chinese coolies there, and Yung Wing's indignation over the
situation. Later, however, the time came when this early interest
in Chinese problems, and friendship with Yung Wing and others
in the Chinese delegation, would result in a situation in which
these men would be instrumental in helping to improve conditions in Peru. (Yung Wings's official report to his own government had resulted in the end of the sending of coolies to
work in Peru.)

In 1880, however, the less progressive of the two parties in the
Chinese government came into power and recalled the students
from New England, most of whom had not yet completed their
education. Yung Wing, who had worked hard on this educational
mission, was greatly disappointed and tried to prevent such a
disaster. First, he got a petition signed by college presidents in
whose institutions the Chinese students were enrolled, explaining
what progress the students were making, and why the closing of
the mission would be regrettable.

Yung Wing wanted a more prominent person to help with
this problem with his own government, however, and discussed

the matter with Twichell. General Grant had received great honors in China and was much respected there. Twichell went at once to Mark Twain, who knew the general, to make arrangements for a meeting with Grant.

Shortly thereafter, Twichell and Twain went to New York to see Grant, Twichell equipped with a well-prepared statement of the situation. He was ready to discuss the Chinese question in general, and that of the students in particular, in great detail, but never got the chance. Grant was well informed on the whole problem and agreed immediately to write a personal letter to Li Hung-Chang in the Chinese government, showing how the end of the mission would be a mistake.

As a result of Grant's letter, the Chinese authorities reconsidered the situation and reinstated the program, at least temporarily.[19] This problem with the Chinese students, and the cooperative venture which it became for Twichell and Twain, is typical of the way in which, together, they often worked on problems of civic interest in the community.

This was also true of their participation in national politics the year of the Cleveland-Blaine presidential election. What actually happened was that during October, 1884, several newspapers in Connecticut carried an article, headlined:

To the Republican Voters of Connecticut

The Republican party has placed in nomination for the highest office in the gift of the people a man against whose past official record there are grave accusations. . . .

Mr. Blaine occupied for many years the position of Speaker of the House of Representatives—a position whose occupant has far greater power than any other person to shape legislation, to further, modify or thwart measures, and to favor or defeat jobs and private schemes. The speaker can serve the public as no other officer can, or he can serve the interests of himself and his friends. Mr. Caldwell stated the case correctly when he wrote to Mr. Fisher in 1871: "Blaine is an important man for us to have feel all right towards us." . . .

Some of us will emphasize our protest by voting for Mr. Cleveland; some of us think we shall do our duty by not voting at all for presidential electors; but we all unite in calling upon our fellow-republicans in this state, which has ever been the home of honest government, to give no vote for Mr. Blaine.[20]

The article was signed by 101 people from all over Connecticut, including T. R. Lounsbury of New Haven, and S. L. Clemens and

J. H. Twichell of Hartford. As it actually happened it is not so interesting a story as Twain later made it by inventing the tale of Twichell's almost losing his church because of the statement in the paper and because his Republican parishioners would not put up with his declaration that he was not going to vote a straight ticket. But this was Twain's imagination at work. The only actual adverse reaction was one letter in the "Letters from the People" column in the *Courant* regretting that a minister should express a political opinion instead of sticking to his theological concerns! In its more prosaic actuality, the incident is simply one of many which indicate the collaboration of Twain and Twichell in community affairs.

The non-professional and non-business activities in which Mark Twain did participate in Hartford were almost completely in company with Twichell. An important part of Twichell's influence on him during these years is, thus, his leading him into affairs which were of interest to both. Twain does not seem to have made many other social connections in the city.

He did not enter into the activities of an organization of which he had previously been an interested member. While still a Mississippi River pilot, Twain had become a Mason. On December 26, 1860, he petitioned for membership in Polar Star Lodge, Number 79, of St. Louis, Missouri, stating his desire to be a candidate for membership, and promising "to conform to all the ancient established usages and customs of the fraternity." He was recommended by John M. Leavenworth and Tom Moore. The petition was received on the same day, and the committee made a favorable report on February 18, 1861. He was initiated and took his first degree on May 21, 1861; second degree, June 12, 1861; and third degree, July 10, 1861.

Even after he left the Mississippi River, Twain continued to be interested in Masonry. During the trip which he made to Palestine in 1866, he sent his lodge at St. Louis a mallet accompanied by the following memorandum:

> This mallet is made of cedar cut in the forest of Lebanon whence Solomon obtained the timber for the Temple. The handle was cut by Brother Clemens himself from a cedar planted just outside the walls of Jerusalem by Brother Godfrey DeBoullion, the first Christian conqueror of that city, 19 July 1099. The gavel in its present form was made at Alexandria, Egypt, by order of Brother Clemens.[21]

In 1869 he requested a demit from the lodge in Missouri, knowing that he preferred to live in the East. His desire to leave his original lodge in good standing would seem to indicate that he planned to re-affiliate with another lodge when he had settled down in his eastern residence. Investigation of Masonic records in Connecticut and New York gives no evidence that he ever placed his demit in any lodge in these states requesting reinstatement into the organization as an active member.[22] In Hartford, Twain's social contacts were almost completely with the Nook Farm community, and he did not have to look outside that group for social activities. There were many Masonic activities in Hartford in which he could have participated, but with an already full schedule, it is probable that Twain just never became interested.

The friendship which began with the meeting of the two men in 1867 grew through the years to include friendship between their families and among their other friends. In its three aspects, different interests of each man were foremost. Always there were the characteristics which they shared in common and could enjoy together—the boyish enthusiasm always present in their personal relationship, their love of their families in the companionship shared by the families, and the civic-minded spirit possessed by both which is evidenced in their participation in community problems. Men who liked each other, who were fond of their wives and children, and who had a serious concern about human nature and man in society, they shared many things during their association with each other.

Although there is often a stiffness and formality in most of Twichell's published statements about Twain, he was undoubtedly sincere in his remarks in the *Courant* in a letter which he wrote the day after Twain's death. While, as usual, he omitted the more personal part of his real liking for the man, he did show what his estimate of him was. The letter was written shortly before Twichell left for New York to conduct the funeral service for his long-time friend.

> The word which came last evening, that the struggle at Redding, which we all had been watching with bated breath, was over, was not unexpected; yet was not without the effect of a shock, as such word ever is. We had not been able to make it seem real that Mark Twain was dying. With me it brought the tide of memories that had been rising ever since I heard how desperately sick he was, to the flood. . . .

Along with his penetrating insight of the weaknesses of humanity went an equally keen appreciation of its nobler aspects and capabilities. What was honorable he most heartily honored. He was not wanting in generous tolerations, high admirations, deep reverences, yes, and deep humilities. No one could be much in his company without perceiving that he was of a singularly affectionate nature. He was quickly responsive to any appeal to his sympathy, especially to his pity. I have seldom known a person so easily moved to tears. He could sometimes be of an unsparingly hostile temper toward a fellow man, but he could never bear to see an animal in pain.

In the retrospect of the more than forty years in which I shared his friendship, and during which in a wide diversity of scenes and circumstances he and I spent much time together, I find that nothing about him is more deeply graven in my memory than that which illustrates the kindly side of his character, which from first to last made him to me above everything else, lovable.

His home life, as all who were observant of it will bear witness, was happy beyond measure. He was the most devoted of husbands and fathers. His fireside was the dearest place to him in all the world. His desolation by successive domestic bereavements was pathetic in the extreme. With all his brilliant prosperities he had lived to be a lonely, weary-hearted man, and the thought of his departure hence was not unwelcome to him.

Joseph H. Twichell[23]

VIII

⚜

Twichell and Twain: Religious Activities and Attitudes

MANY MISCONCEPTIONS have appeared in discussions of Twain's attitude toward Twichell's religion and his church in Hartford. Statements by contemporary observers have led to the belief that, while the two men were friends, they disagreed so completely on religious ideas that Twichell's ministry was a separate part of his life from that in which Twain was a part, and something in which Twain did not participate even in conversation. That this idea is prevalent among literary critics and biographers is understandable when the statements by two of their contemporaries, men who knew them well and should have been accurate, are noted.

Writing in 1910, the year of Twain's death, William Dean Howells, who had been very closely associated with both men for a long period of years, said:

> . . . He still loved his old friend and pastor, Mr. Twichell, but he no longer went to hear him preach his sane and beautiful sermons, and was, I think, thereby the greater loser. Long before that I had asked him if he went regularly to church, and he groaned out: "Oh yes, I go. It 'most kills me, but I go," and I did not need his telling me to understand that he went because his wife wished it. He did tell me after they both ceased to go that it had finally come to her saying, "Well, if you are to be lost, I want to be lost with you."[1]

The second misleading statement came from A. B. Paine, Twain's official biographer, who spent much time with him in the later years. In his *Mark Twain, a Biography,* Paine said that up until the time of the European trip about which Twain wrote *A Tramp Abroad,* they had discussed religion, but one day as they were hiking, Twain said to Twichell:

"Joe, . . . I'm going to make a confession. I don't believe in
your religion at all. I've been living a lie right straight along
whenever I pretended to. For a moment, sometimes, I have been
almost a believer, but it immediately drifts away from me again.
I don't believe one word of your Bible was inspired by God any
more than any other book. I believe it is entirely the work of
man from beginning to end—atonement and all. The problem of
life and death and eternity and the true conception of God is a
bigger thing than is contained in that book."

Paine adds, significantly, "So the personal side of religious discussion closed between them, and was never afterward reopened."[2]

It is impossible to dismiss the subject with the comments of
just two people, however, even though those two should have
known what they were talking about. There is much evidence,
moreover, that would indicate that such a break in their discussions of religion never occurred, and that Mark Twain did
continue to attend the Asylum Hill Congregational Church as
long as he lived in Hartford.

This matter of their religious conversations and activities together is extremely important and must be established firmly
before any literary influence can be estimated; because if such
literary influence exists, it must come, at least in part, from the
most basic part of Twichell's life, his ministry and his attitudes
and beliefs as a Christian pastor. If he did not influence Twain in
that respect, which would of necessity be true if they never discussed the personal side of religion, then his total effect on Twain
the author would be of relatively little significance.

The evidence points, however, to disagreement with both William Dean Howells and A. B. Paine. The religious aspect of the
friendship may be seen to be an important factor in their relationship throughout their lives.

First of all, the Clemens family did participate in the activities
of Twichell's church. Secondly, Twichell often adopted the attitude of pastor toward parishioner in the relationship with Twain,
and Mark Twain seems to have accepted this attitude completely.

Twain began to attend Twichell's church on his early visits
to Hartford when he first met Joe, and some time before he
himself moved to Hartford. Because the church included many
important people in its congregation from its founding, newspapers in cities as far away as Boston and New York sent reporters to attend a Sunday service and to write an article on the
church building and its dignitaries in attendance. Twichell, the

new young minister, was impressed with these articles as they appeared and carefully preserved copies of them in his scrapbook, correcting in the margin any errors made by the reporters.

In these clippings, the presence of the political and literary figures was always emphasized by the writers, who consistently noted Mark Twain's presence. The form of these articles seldom varied. The reporter would go to Hartford where he knew at least one member of the church. Attending the service with his friend, the reporter would have pointed out to him and would, accordingly, record in his article, the celebrities in attendance.

The following is typical of the attention always paid to Mark Twain's presence.

> Just before the service begins Charles Dudley Warner, who is winning fame as one of our most brilliant writers walks quickly up near the pulpit, treading lightly as if afraid of disturbing the congregation. I liked his appearance as well as I liked his My Summer in a Garden, one of the most quietly humorous books ever written. Mr. Warner, who is one of the editors of the Courant, is apparently about forty years old, dressed in rather a careless manner and wears glasses. Directly behind him appears a man, dressed in furs, with a rather awkward hesitating manner as if he wasn't sure where his pew was located; his locks were rather curly over a somewhat low forehead, but, after all, he was one concerning whom a stranger would say, as did I, "Who is that?" and the answer would be "Why, don't you know? Mark Twain!" Sure enough, it was that celebrated humorist who has made so many laugh on both sides of the water, and out of both corners of the mouth.[3]

Over and over such reports appeared in one newspaper after another for many years, this one merely being a sample of many.

There is evidence scattered through Twichell's scrapbooks indicating that Mark Twain took part regularly in the activities of the church, contributed to many of the causes which the church was supporting, and contributed his services several times to help raise money for the church itself.

In 1875, for example, the young people of the Asylum Hill Church planned a festival to raise money. One of the attractions was to be a spelling bee. When it was announced that contestants would include Mark Twain, Twichell, Judge Carpenter, General Hawley, the Rev. Dr. Burton, and others equally well known to Hartford people, the church was so crowded that the audience had to move from the chapel to the main auditorium. After the contestants were seated on the platform, Twichell called on Twain for a few preliminary remarks. Twain responded with a brief and delightfully amusing talk about spelling.

Twain concluded his remarks by saying, "The insurrection will now begin." Judge Carpenter was the first to fail, spelling *gizzard* with one *z*; Twichell put two *l's* in *pelisse*; General Hawley missed *trisyllable*. Twain himself, always a good speller, survived for some time, but finally missed on *chaldron,* which he spelled *cauldron*. After the match a check in the dictionary proved that Twain had been correct, his spelling being listed as another "in current usage." He registered no official protest, however, because he had provided the prizes: a five-volume *History of France,* a nosegay painted on slate, and the London Art Journal for 1875, from among which the winner was to choose. A Miss Stone was the victor and selected the nosegay. Since Judge Carpenter had been the first speller to miss a word, Mark Twain presented him with a box of children's colored blocks, on which the letters of the alphabet were painted.[4]

The young people who had sponsored the affair were delighted with the $600 which was raised. Just as important was the pleasant evening which Asylum Hill Church people and their friends had enjoyed—and Mark Twain was certainly an active participant.

On May 31, 1876, there was an evening program, a concert by the Park Church Quintette and readings by Mark Twain in the chapel of the Asylum Hill Church. From this evening only the announcement has survived, so that even the program itself cannot be discovered. What the Quintette sang, and what Mark Twain read can only be guessed, but it is evident from these examples that Twain did participate in various church activities.

In 1888, the church presented the Twichells with the deed of their house. They had collected $10,000, the additional $4,000 beyond the amount needed for the house to be used for improvements. Twichell, who had suspected that his fiftieth birthday was to receive some sort of recognition had, he said, thought that it would take the shape of crockery. One of the men present said that Twichell's "first remarks were a series of exclamation points."[5]

The presentation of the house was made on Twichell's birthday, May 27: the next evening the church held a reception for the Twichells. The first speaker of the evening made some remarks on the progress of the world during Twichell's fifty years of existence. Then the house was formally presented.

Mark Twain was the next speaker. The *Courant* reported on the next day:

> Mr. S. L. Clemens, who followed, said that he supposed he had been called partly because he was a considerable portion of the congregation. He stood as evidence of what Mr. Twichell had been able to construct. He was glad to learn from the first speaker, Mr. Allen, that Mr. Twichell was largely accountable for the progress the world has made during the past 50 years. Until he had spoken he had never realized that the telegraph and the telephone and all those things were due to the influence of this man—the handsomest man that ever lived. We all feel alike, continued Mr. Clemens, about the limitless degree of affection expressed in the paper read by Mr. Morris and hope it will be kept up so long as Mr. Twichell continues to do so well. Mr. Clemens then related an absurb incident which had occurred in Switzerland, showing how great an influence Mr. Twichell had exerted upon him during their sojourn in that country, and closed by reading the following poem, which, he said, reminded him so strongly of his pastor:—Days of my youth, Ye have glided away; . . .[6]

The date of this talk, May 28, 1888, is significant in view of Howells' statement that as late as this, Twain was no longer having anything to do with the church. If he had not been, it hardly seems likely that the church people would have considered asking him to take part in this ceremony, even though he was Twichell's friend. The mere fact of his being asked to participate would indicate that his relations with the church and its members, as well as the minister, were still very good. It can, likewise, hardly be assumed that they invited him simply because he was a famous man who would add prestige to their program. Of celebrities and dignitaries in various occupations they had a good supply. It was, nevertheless, Twain whom they wanted to speak at this service which was completely a church affair, in honor of the pastor. His presence was taken for granted and he was happy to attend and to speak.

Twain's participation in such church activities and his attendance at Sunday services seem also to have been taken for granted by the Hartford papers of the time. References are more difficult to find, therefore, than if it had been a newsworthy event every time he went to church or took part in a parish function. In Hartford Twain was, first of all, "Mr. S. L. Clemens of Farmington Avenue," as the papers usually referred to him. No one seems to have been surprised, therefore, to find him, with his family, an active participant in church activities.

While reporters from out of town thought it worth mentioning that they had seen Mark Twain in church, the Hartford papers mentioned mostly the additional things like the spelling bee, the readings, the speech at Twichell's reception, and similar matters. Both his and his wife's names appeared also in groups of people taking part in some activity, but simply in lists of other names, not as headlines—Mrs. Clemens, for example, on the decoration committee of the church on several occasions, and similar kinds of every-day participation in the events of the church.

It was only after Twain's death that Hartford people began to realize that there had been anything of news value in such matters. But even then, his regular attendance at church was taken for granted, not by Howells at a distance, or by Paine writing in the years shortly before Twain's death, but by men who had actually been present at the time.

In 1912, Edwin Pond Parker wrote several articles for the *Courant* about his relationship with Twain, whom he had rather stuffily advised at one time, he admitted, to stay with more serious writing. The following is typical of the kind of report that appeared after Twain's Hartford residence had come to an end. Perhaps, also, during his long years of living in Hartford, people had simply respected his privacy to some extent. Writing in the *Courant*, Parker said:

> Having mentioned Mr. Clemens's enjoyment of music, I am reminded of what occurred one Sunday morning in the church of which I was then the minister. Congregational singing prevailed in Dr. Twichell's church, at that time, while the South Church had a fine choir of which it was justly proud. Now and then, when Dr. Twichell was absent, Mr. and Mrs. Clemens would stray away from their accustomed place of worship and come to the South Church, to hear—as he was fond of telling me—the music there. Accordingly, one Sunday forenoon he so came and he and his wife were seated in the pastor's pew. In due time the ushers proceeded to "take up the collection," a part of the service for which he was not prepared. He saw them approaching him, and looked to his wife for relief. She was unable to assist him and shook her head, to that effect. There was no time for reflection, for the crisis was at hand. He met it heroically and in an original manner, for as the plate was thrust toward him, he looked calmly up to the young man who held it, and hoarsely whispered, "Charge it, please!" The young usher

nearly had a fit, and some who overheard that whisper forgot for a while the solemnity of the sanctuary.[7]

In attempting to indicate Twain's continued attendance at Twichell's church, it is apparent that the amusing anecdote related by Parker is not so valuable as the simple statement, "Now and then, when Dr. Twichell was absent, Mr. and Mrs. Clemens would stray away from their accustomed place of worship and come to the South Church." While the Clemens family lived in Hartford, Asylum Hill Congregational Church was always their "accustomed place of worship," and that fact was calmly accepted by those on the scene, like Parker, along with the fact that "now and then," they went elsewhere.

Parker concluded his article by telling of his first evening with Twain in the 1860's when Twichell had introduced them. He recounted one of the stories told by Twain on that occasion, one about a minister in a mining camp who won the hearts of the men. Suggesting that the name of the camp should be changed, the minister was not sure that he had accomplished what he wanted to, when the men did change the name—from Devil's Gulch to Jehovah Gap.

Parker concluded his discussion:

> In one of his poems, Mr. Emerson speaks of hearing a bird sing at morning in an entrancing way.
>
> > "I brought him home, in his nest, at even,
> > He sings the song, but it cheers not now,
> > For I did not bring the river and sky."
>
> It is so with the old story, for I have not brought, could not bring home with it Mark Twain's inimitable narration of it. What the river and the sky and the dawn and the alder bough were to the sparrow's song, Mr. Clemens's manner, method, personality and atmosphere were to all his various stories. In this minor and (as I suppose) hitherto unpublished one, there was no suggestion, as he told it, of an irreverence, but contrariwise, it smacked of a rough, honest, though somewhat droll and surprising effect toward piety and propriety.
>
> May it please Dr. Twichell to pardon me this trespass and these few gleanings in a harvest-field that really belongs to him.[8]

Besides the formal connection with the church, and participation in its activities, Mark Twain also discussed religion with Twichell and very definitely considered him his pastor as well as his friend. This aspect of the friendship appears usually when

Mark Twain was emotionally disturbed, perhaps about the deaths of his daughters Susan and Jean, or his wife. At those times, Twichell talked to him, or wrote to him if he were at a distance, and the substance and general tone of the letters indicate that discussion of spiritual matters was often part of their conversations.

In the very early years of their friendship when there was little need for this kind of consolation from Twichell, religion could even provide material for laughter between them.

In 1877, on their first trip to Bermuda, Twain decided that Bermuda was one of the best places he had ever visited.

Finally, he said, "Joe, this place is like Heaven, and I'm going to make the most of it."

Twichell replied, "Mark, that's right; make the most of a place *like* Heaven while you have a chance."[9]

There were always, also, the theoretical discussions of matters like moral responsibility between them. Twichell, disciple of Horace Bushnell, with the years of Congregational tradition behind him could never accept Mark Twain's deterministic belief that man is not responsible for what he does. That man deserves neither credit nor blame for his actions, that he is motivated only by selfish desires were ideas which Twichell did not believe— just as Twain disagreed with Twichell's more traditional, Christian approach. This subject came up over and over again, but always as discussion, not argument: personalities were not involved; ideas were. It was obvious from the beginning that neither would ever convince the other of the falsity of his beliefs, but they could not let the subject alone.

When Twichell pointed out something good which Twain himself had accomplished and for which he deserved credit, Twain merely told him that he did not recognize the selfish motives in back of it all, but that such motives were really present. This kind of argument can never come to a satisfactory conclusion for the participants, but it can continue indefinitely, which it did with these two. Primarily, it provided many hours of challenging conversation, and between meetings, both men tried hard to gather evidence from things they saw, books they read, and conversations they had with others. Armed with new equipment, they were delighted to start the subject all over again at any opportunity.

As A. B. Paine and others have pointed out, and as Twichell's son, Joseph Hooker Twichell, confirms, Twain and Twichell were both very much interested in the "human critter," and this was their common starting point. About this "critter," they disagreed on much. While Twichell saw man as a species growing better and better, with biological evolution leading also to spiritual improvement, Twain saw man as a species as not worth much at present, and certainly not getting any better—but they could agree on individuals, and they were both deeply concerned with the individual personality as they saw it manifested in people they knew.

While these arguments were often repetitious statements of what each already believed and had said before, they sometimes found ammunition in the writings of other men and presented it to each other with glee. On one occasion, Twichell lent Twain his copy of Jonathan Edwards' *Freedom of the Will* for perusal on a train trip. Although far from agreeing with Edwards himself, he thought he had found in him ideas similar to Twain's which would provide excellent food for later discussion. (This occurred long after the *Tramp Abroad* trip, and, in spite of Paine's statement to the contrary, they were still talking about religion. Paine, apparently not recognizing the contradiction which he was establishing in his own work, included the letter in his *Biography*.)

Twichell was right in thinking that Twain would be interested in the book, which he had not happened to read previously. Twain wrote to him the next day, beginning:

> From Bridgeport to New York, thence to home, & continuously until near midnight I wallowed & reeked with Jonathan in his insane debauch; rose immensely refreshed & fine at ten this morning, but with a strange & haunting sense of having been on a three days' tear with a drunken lunatic. It is years since I have known these sensations. All through the book is the glare of a resplendent intellect gone mad—a marvelous spectacle. No, not *all* through the book—the drunk does not come on till the last third, where what I take to be Calvinism & its God begins to show up & shine red & hideous in the glow from the fires of hell, their only right and proper adornment.
>
> Jonathan seems to hold (as against the Arminian position) that the man (or his soul or his will) never *creates* an impulse itself, but is moved to action by an impulse back of it. That's sound!
>
> Also, that of two or more things offered, it infallibly chooses the one which for the moment is most *pleasing* to ITSELF. *Perfectly* correct! An immense admission for a man not otherwise sane.
>
> Up to that point he could have written Chapters III & IV of my suppressed *Gospel*. But there we seem to separate. . . .

The point of separation was that of man's responsibility to God
for his actions. If man never created an impulse himself, but was
governed by Necessity (forces over which the man had no control), then Twain could not accept the fact that the man was at all
responsible to anyone for what he did. And on that point, he considered Edwards' ideas to be so contradictory that they were, to
him, insane.

Twain continued:

> I think that when he concedes the autocratic dominion to
> Motive and Necessity he grants a *third* position of mine—that a
> man's mind is a mere machine—an automatic machine—which is
> handled entirely from the *outside,* the man himself furnishing it
> absolutely nothing; not an ounce for its fuel, & not so much as
> bare *suggestion* to that exterior engineer as to what the machine
> shall do nor *how* it shall do it nor *when.*
>
> After that concession it was time for him to get alarmed & *shirk*
> —for he was pointed straight for the only rational & possible next
> station on *that* piece of road—the irresponsibility of man to God.
>
> And so he shirked. Shirked, and arrived at this handsome result.
>
> Man is commanded to do so & so.
>
> It has been ordained from the beginning of time that some men
> sha'nt & others can't.
>
> *These are to blame: let them be damned.*
>
> I enjoy the Colonel very much, & shall enjoy the rest of him
> with an obscene delight.
>
> Joe, the whole tribe shout love to you & yours.[10]

That last sentence in the letter, irrelevant to the matter at hand,
becomes very important. After his long philosophical and theological discussion, Twain ended the letter in a lightly jovial fashion. The letter itself is very typical, then, of the spirit of many
of these discussions—heated and sincere presentations of different
points of view in a warm, friendly manner.

Besides the church activities in which Mark Twain participated
actively, and the conversations in which, apparently, neither convinced the other of anything, there were also many occasions on
which Twichell acted very decidedly as the family pastor as well
as family friend. There were the usual times when a minister is
needed: the Clemens' wedding soon after Joe and Mark met,
Susy's death and funeral in 1896, Mrs. Clemens' funeral in 1904,
Jean's in 1909, Clara's wedding to Ossip Gabrilowitsch in 1910,
and, finally, the funeral service for Twain himself in 1910.

The deaths of his daughters and his wife were blows from which Mark Twain had a hard time recuperating. Always Twichell tried to help him, usually by letters in the later years when they were no longer living close together in Hartford. It is evident that Mark Twain accepted Twichell's help, and even sought it, even though it was not always so effective as either might have wished. The fact that Joe tried to console Mark through correspondence is significantly indicative of the presence of this kind of relationship in their friendship. What he probably would have been able to do, what he had often done when they lived close together, he tried desperately to do from a distance. Mark Twain obviously appreciated what Twichell was trying to do.

One of the most serious blows to Twain was the death of his daughter Susan in Hartford, while the rest of the family was in Europe. When he heard of Susan's illness, Twichell immediately left the White Mountains where he was staying and returned to Hartford.

After she died, Twichell, with a few other friends, went to New York to meet Mrs. Clemens and Clara, who were trying to get home before Susan died. These men even went so far as to hire a tugboat in order to meet the incoming vessel at night before it docked, and to be with Mrs. Clemens and Clara on the last lap of their journey, to help them return to Hartford, and to offer any assistance possible. The origin of the tugboat idea was Twichell's and is an interesting revelation of his thoughtfulness and resourcefulness. On the boat, he first found Clara, who knew what had happened as soon as she saw him and, with his help, went immediately to tell her mother.

This kind of friendship Twain accepted as it was offered; and in matters like this, Joe was much more the spiritual friend and pastor than the jovial hiking companion who has been so often pictured.

As soon as he learned what had happened, Mark Twain wrote to Twichell:

> Through Livy and Katy I have learned, dear old Joe, how loyally you stood poor Susy's friend, and mine, and Livy's; how you came all the way down, twice, from your summer refuge on your merciful errands to bring the peace and comfort of your beloved presence, first to that poor child, and again to the broken heart of her poor desolate mother. It was like you; like your good great heart, like your matchless and unmatchable self. It was no

surprise to me to learn that you stayed by Susy long hours, careless
of fatigue and heat, it was no surprise to me to learn that you
could still the storms that swept her spirit when no other could;
for she loved you, revered you, trusted you, and "Uncle Joe" was
no empty phrase upon her lips! I am grateful to you, Joe, grateful
to the bottom of my heart, which has always been filled with love
for you, and respect and admiration; and I would have chosen
you out of all the world to take my place at Susy's side and Livy's
in those black hours.

Susy was a rare creature; the rarest that has been reared in Hartford in this generation. And Livy knew it, and you knew it, and
Charley Warner and George, and Harmony, and the Hillyers and
the Dunhams and the Cheneys, and Dick Burton, and perhaps
others. And I also was of the number, but not in the same degree—
for she was above my duller comprehension. I merely knew that
she was my superior in fineness of mind; in the delicacy and
subtlety of her intellect, but to fully measure her I was not com-
petent. I know her better now; for I have read her private writings
and sounded the deeps of her mind; and I know better, now, the
treasure that was mine than I knew it when I had it. But I have
this consolation; that dull as I was, I always knew enough to be
proud when she commended me or my work—as proud as if Livy
had done it herself—and I took it as the accolade from the hand
of genius. I see now—as Livy always saw—that she had greatness
in her; and that she herself was dimly conscious of it.

And now she is dead—and I can never tell her.

God bless you Joe—and all of your house.[11]

During the next few months, after Mrs. Clemens and Clara
had returned to England, Twichell attempted further consolation
of the heart-broken family by mail, but Twain himself was particularly inconsolable. His emotional tendency to blame himself
for things that had happened (in spite of his theoretical "man is
not responsible"), his great love for his family, and the general
gloom that was beginning to cast its spell over his later years had
begun to overpower him. His answers to Twichell's letters, finally,
even apparently gave Twichell the idea that Twain did not want
to receive any more of his kind of Christian consolation. As close
friends can do, he asked him very frankly if he wanted to continue
receiving letters from him.

Twain responded:

DEAR JOE,—Do I want you to write to me? Indeed I do. I do
not want most people to write, but I do want you to do it. The
others break my heart, but you will not. You have a something in

you that is not in other men. You have the touch that heals, not lacerates. And you know the secret places of our hearts. You know our life—the outside of it—as the others do—and the inside of it— which they do not. You have seen our whole voyage. You have seen us go to sea, a cloud of sail, and the flag at the peak; and you see us now, chartless, adrift—derelicts; battered, water-logged, our sails a ruck of rags, our pride gone. For it is gone. And there is nothing in its place. The vanity of life was all we had, and there is no more vanity left in us. We are even ashamed at that we had; ashamed that we trusted the promises of life and builded high—to come to this!

He continued, as he so often did in letters to Twichell, express-ing his inner feelings, asking questions, and "talking out" in writ-ing the thoughts that were overflowing his mind. Twichell was more than an understanding listener in this situation; he was also more than a friend; here he was the minister, the parson, and to him, as to no other person, Twain could bare his soul.

I did know that Susy was part of us; I did *not* know that she could go away; I did not know that she could go away and take our lives with her, yet leave our dull bodies behind. And I did not know what she was. To me she was but treasure in the bank, the amount known, the need to look at it daily, handle it, weigh it, count it, *realize* it, not necessary; and now that I could do it, it is too late; they tell me it is not there, has vanished away in a night, the bank is broken, my fortune is gone, I am a pauper. How am I to comprehend this? How am I to *have* it? Why am I robbed, and who is benefited?

Ah, well, Susy died at *home*. She had that privilege. Her dying eyes rested upon nothing that was strange to them, but only upon things which they had known and loved always and which had made her young years glad; and she had you, and Sue, and Katy, and John, and Ellen. This was happy fortune—I am thankful that it was vouch-safed to her. If she had died in another house—well, I think I could not have borne that. To us, our house was not unsentient matter— it had a heart, and a soul, and eyes to see us with; and approvals and solicitudes, and deep sympathies; it was of us, and we were in its confidence, and lived in its grace and in the peace of its bene-diction. We never came home from an absence that its face did not light up and speak out its eloquent welcome—and we could not enter it unmoved. And could we now, oh, now, in spirit we should enter it unshod.

Twichell had apparently attempted to console the grieving father by pointing out his other assets, his remaining blessings, but Twain continued:

I am trying to add to the "assets" which you estimate so generously. No, I am not. The thought is not in my mind. My purpose is other. I am working, but it is for the sake of the work—the "surcease of sorrow" that is found there. I work all the days, and trouble vanishes away when I use that magic. This book will not long stand between it and me, now; but that is no matter. I have many unwritten books to fly to for my preservation; the interval between the finishing of this one and the beginning of the next will not be more than an hour, at most. *Continuances,* I mean; for two of them are already well along—in fact have reached exactly the same stage in their journey: 19,000 words each. The present one will contain 180,000 words—130,000 are done. I am well protected; but Livy! She has nothing in the world to turn to; nothing but housekeeping, and doing things for the children and me. She does not see people, and cannot; books have lost their interest for her. She sits solitary; and all the day, and all the days, wonders how it all happened, and why. We others were always busy with our affairs, but Susy was her comrade—had to be driven from her loving persecutions—sometimes at 1 in the morning. To Livy the persecutions were welcome. It was heaven to her to be plagued like that. But it is ended now. Livy stands so in need of help; and none among us could help her like you.

Although Twain recognized that Twichell could help Livy, Twichell could not be there to help either one of them. If he could have been, he might have been able to do some good. Twain, at least, certainly felt that he could. He concluded:

Some day you and I will walk again, Joe and talk. I hope so. We could have *such* talks! We are all grateful to you and Harmony—*how* grateful it is not given to us to say in words. We pay as we can, in love; and in this coin practicing no economy. Good bye, dear old Joe![12]

It does not seem possible to question the sincerity of the letters written by Twain at this time. This was not Twain the author writing what he knew the audience wanted; this was not Twain the friend writing newsy letters; this was a bereaved father writing to a close friend and pastor. In this group of letters concerning Susy's death, he was not seeking the diplomatic thing to say, the thing that the correspondent would want to hear—or he would not have said to a father of nine children that Susy was the "rarest creature that has been reared in Hartford in this generation." He was writing what he felt.

Twichell was always the one to whom Twain wrote when he was upset. That this was true because of the personality of Twichell and their close friendship rather than because of his being a minister may, undoubtedly, be true; but Twichell's sympathetic and understanding nature was so integrally a part of his pastoral qualities that here, too, may be seen Twain's acceptance of the fact that this man was also his pastor. The fact that in formal theology they could never agree made no difference when the time came and Twain needed someone to write to with complete freedom. He could rest assured that whatever he said would be taken in good spirit, and there was apparently always an unspoken hope that, perhaps, his friend would have an answer.

Twain himself was aware that he was using his correspondence with Twichell in this way and admitted it to him. In 1905, he concluded a letter by saying:

> I have written to you to-day, not to do you a service, but to do myself one. There was bile in me. I had to empty it or lose my day to-morrow. If I tried to empty it into the *North American Review*—oh, well, I couldn't afford the risk. No, the certainty! The certainty that I wouldn't be satisfied with the result; so I would burn it, & try again to-morrow; burn that and try again the next day. It happens so nearly every time. I have a family to support, & I can't afford this kind of dissipation. Last winter when I was sick I wrote a magazine article three times before I got it to suit me. I put $500 worth of work on it every day for ten days, & at last when I got it to suit me it contained but 3,000 words—$900. I burned it & said I would reform.
>
> And I *have* reformed. I *have* to work my bile off whenever it gets to where I can't stand it, but I can work it off on you economically, because I don't have to make it suit me. It may not suit you, but that isn't any matter; I'm not writing for that. I have used you as an equilibrium-restorer more than once in my time, & shall continue, I guess, I would like to use Mr. Rogers, & he is plenty good-natured enough, but it wouldn't be fair to keep him rescuing me from my leather-headed business snarls & make him read interminable bile-irruptions besides; I can't use Howells, he is busy & old & lazy, & won't stand it; I dasn't use Clara, there's things I have to say which she wouldn't put up with—a very dear little ashcat, but has claws.
> And so—you're It.[13]

What Twichell said to be helpful in Twain's bleaker moments seems to have contained two main currents of thought: the first, the sympathy and understanding of a friend; but second, also, the recommendation of help that might come from greater spiritual powers. Even though Paine said that in 1878 they ended all dis-

cussion of the personal aspect of religion, the correspondence between them would seem to indicate that this was not so, as would
Twichell's later comments about Twain. In one speech, for example, Twichell added to his retelling of anecdotes now familiar,
"It is not amiss for me to recall here—that we said our prayers
together."[14]

The death of Mrs. Clemens brought to Twain both of the kinds
of consolation Joe had to offer. Immediately upon hearing of her
death, the Twichells wrote simply:

DEAR, DEAR MARK,—There is nothing we can say. What is
there *to* say? But here we are—with you all every hour and every
minute—filled with unutterable thoughts; unutterable affection for
the dead and for the living.

HARMONY AND JOE[15]

As minister, Twichell went to Elmira for the funeral. Mark
Twain wrote in his notes:

July 14, 1904 (ELMIRA). Funeral private in the house of
Livy's young maidenhood. Where she stood as a bride 34 years ago
there her coffin rested; & over it the same voice that had made her
a wife then committed her spirit to God now.[16]

Again, as he had after Susy's death, Mark Twain wrote to Twichell asking *why?* Twichell's response seems to be one of the most
significant available in its indication of the kind of aid he offered.
Its thoughts, meaning, and tone all illustrate well this aspect of
the friendship.

About a month after Livy's death, Twichell wrote:

I can't wonder—and I don't—that with the light of your life gone
out you sit dazed in the dark seeing no meaning or reason in anything, the Universe appearing to you only a confusion of unin-
telligible phantasmagoria. But it makes my heart ache for you,
old fellow. I wish I was with you—why I hardly know—I have
nothing to *say* to you; not now; but I would like to be where you
are, and have you in sight, and wander about with you, silent or
talking or what not. For I am not ignorant of the thoughts you
are thinking. They have visited me, too. I, indeed, believe, that
behind the riddle there is a Hidden and Awful Wisdom; that for
one tempest-tossed in these wide weltering seas there is an An-
chorage, that for the mortal spirit there is a practicable victory
over the world with all its baffling mysteries.

Of course I do, or I wouldn't be a Christian minister. But I am
not going to preach to you. I don't feel in the least like it. I

would, though, as I say, like mightily to be at your side just now. May be, Mark, we would kneel together once in a while, as we have done in times past. Really, it seems to me, that is the posture for a man to take in the midst of these unfathomable realities.[17]

Why Paine and Howells, who knew both men, should have misunderstood the nature of the religious aspect of their friendship seems difficult to determine. In the above letter, Twichell's "we would kneel together once in a while, as we have done in times past," would certainly prove without question that there was no cessation of the personal aspect of religion between them. If there had been such a conclusion between them at any time in the past, Twichell would certainly not have made this statement at this time—and the time was 1904, only six years before Twain's death.

It seems possible that Paine, who knew Twain only in the later years, was never completely sure when he could believe him and when Twain was either being entertaining or forgetful, or giving past facts to coincide with his feelings of the moment, whether true or not. Paine was, apparently, a good listener, and with such a good audience, Twain could hardly resist the temptation to entertain, amuse, startle, and even shock him. As for Howells' misunderstanding of the religious situation, there are several possible reasons which might explain it. Although a good friend, Howells was not always on the scene in Hartford to witness Twain's participation in the activities of the Asylum Hill Church, nor was he aware of the nature of the long talks and later correspondence of Twain and Twichell. Also Twain may not have discussed with him or anyone else this very personal side of his friendship with Twichell.

More of Twichell's effect on Twain's personality, philosophy, and writing will be discussed in connection with literary matters. There is no doubt, however, that Twain was an active participant in the affairs of the Asylum Hill Congregational Church and attended Sunday services there for many years, that he discussed religious matters of both a personal and theoretical nature with Twichell all during their years as close friends, and that he very often looked to Twichell as his pastor as well as his friend.

Their contemporaries may have misunderstood some aspects of their relationship, but many of them did recognize that there was one side of Twain which Twichell, alone among them, shared. In a letter dated October 19, 1910, William Dean Howells wrote

to Joe—the formal Howells would never have called him Joe any
more than he called Twain, Mark or Sam. In the letter, he said:

> Dear Friend:
>   The American Academy of Arts and Letters will hold a meeting
> in commemoration of our beloved Clemens at Carnegie Music
> Hall on the 30th of November; and we want you to come and
> speak. Do come, and tell some cheerful and happy thing about
> him, with the "light of other days" in it. You knew one side of him
> better than anyone else, and without you, all our good company
> of speakers would be wanting in the best. Say you will come; you
> need not speak more than ten minutes, but you must *look* for an
> hour or two.[18]

While Howells may simply have been attempting to be cordial
in his letter, he and other friends of the two undoubtedly did
recognize that there truly was one side of Twain which Twichell
knew better than did anyone else. But what none of these contemporaries, including probably the families of both, did not have
an opportunity to know was the real nature of that side of Twain
or of Twichell in their relationship together, which included
religion. No one could have listened to their private conversations.
No one until years later could have read their long letters to each
other. These many letters are, indeed, the evidence which proves
many things about both men, which, during their lives, they
shared only with each other.

Edward Wagenknecht in his *Mark Twain: the Man and His
Work* points out that Twichell did not make Mark Twain a
professing Christian. It is true that he never actually joined the
Asylum Hill Congregational Church, even though he was a regular attendant and contributed services and money to the church
and to its missionary endeavors. Twichell seems never to have
tried to persuade him to join, any more than he tried to convert
Father O'Hagan to Protestantism. It is also true that Twain never
agreed with Twichell on many theological and philosophical matters. Much independence of the individual conscience and mind
is a basic fundamental of Congregationalism, however, and there
may well have been actual members of Asylum Hill who also
disagreed with the Bushnellian Twichell. Twain, nevertheless,
was certainly actively involved in the life of the church.

An integral part of the relationship between the two men was
based on the fact of Twichell's Christian ministry and his function
as Mark Twain's pastor as well as his friend.

IX

※

Twichell's Influence on Twain's Writing

WHEN THE SINCERITY and nature of the friendship between Mark Twain and Joseph Hopkins Twichell, in its several aspects, have been realized, it becomes necessary to look for possible influence which Twichell might have exerted on Twain's writing. This is important, also, because of the conclusions drawn in many critical analyses of Twain's writing that Twichell did influence Twain's literary production harmfully by smothering him in an atmosphere of Eastern culture, Puritanism, and respectability, which resulted in repressions of Twain's spontaneity, frontier humor, and independent philosophical thinking.

It is important, first of all, to recognize that Mark Twain sought the advice of the people around him: Livy, Joe, Howells, and often others. This advice was not thrust upon him against his wishes. He sincerely wanted Livy's approval of his writing; as was seen, he delighted in his daughter Susan's approval, and in Joe's.

The reason for this feeling on his part may only be a matter of speculation, but there seems to have been a decided insecurity in Twain's own mind about his writing, just as there was a feeling of unsureness on his part in his early connections with the Eastern people with whom he desperately wanted to take his place.

Twichell pointed out, in one of the letters to his family from Europe, that Twain was the victim of a timidity which made him even apprehensive about the simple matter of approaching strangers. About many things he was unsure, and this element of his personality also entered into his professional life. More than most other authors, he often did not feel at all confident about his own writing and wondered what other people's reactions to it would be—to a degree apparently beyond that of other writers of his ability and standing. Even after he and William Dean Howells had become close enough friends so that Howells would not have

considered reviewing a book of his adversely, a thing which
Howells could never do to a friend, so much the gentleman was
he, Twain was as delighted as a boy with Howells' approval.

In a similar fashion he sought the advice of other men. For
example, he once wrote to Edwin Pond Parker:

> I thank you most sincerely for those pleasant words. They come
> most opportunely, too,—at a time when I was wavering between
> launching a book of the sort you mention, with my name to it,
> and smuggling it into publicity with my name suppressed. Well,
> I'll put my name to it, and let it help me or hurt me as the fates
> shall direct.
>
> It is not a large book, so I have not scrupled to ask Howells
> and Twichell to run over the manuscript and advise me what to
> modify and what to knock out. I must go warily seeing this is
> such a wide departure from my accustomed line.
>
> Howells has read it and he winds up his four pages (mainly of
> vigorous approval) with the remark,—"I think the book will be a
> great success unless some maurading [sic] ass who does not snuff his
> wonted pasturage there, should prevail on all the other asses to
> turn up their noses in pure ignorance. It is such a book as I would
> expect from you, knowing what a bottom of substance there is to
> your fun: but the public at large ought to be led to expect it, and
> must be."
>
> Howells found fault with two things, some descriptions of
> English court ceremonies, which he wants shortened, and a story
> of a boy, a bull, and some bees, which he won't have in the book
> at all, because he says it lowers its dignity, so I guess I'll have to
> snatch that out.
>
> But what I'm coming to is this:—Will you, too, take the manu-
> script and read it, either to yourself, or, still better, aloud, to your
> family? Twichell has promised me a similar service. I hoped to
> get criticism from Howells's children, but evidently he spared
> them, which was carrying charity too far![1]

Livy, Howells, Twichell, Parker, their children—all of these
Twain wanted to read his manuscript before he would have sufficient confidence to send it to his publishers. Certainly no one
was forcing advice on him; he was actively seeking it.

Writing about this letter from Twain, Parker indicated that
he did perform the requested service, but also revealingly, that
Twain did not always accept the advice he had requested when
he was sure himself as to what he wanted to do.

Parker and Twichell were both happily willing to read the
manuscript and did so with enjoyment, but also thoughtfully and

carefully, discussing it in detail with each other and with their families. The book under discussion was *The Prince and the Pauper,* on which Twain had spent much time. On first reading and in later years, both preachers felt that this was one of Twain's best works, though many of the early reviewers, perhaps as Howells had suggested, not finding their "wonted pasturage," paid little attention to it. The story of the boy, the bull, the bees was dropped by Twain before publication, when he found that Parker and Twichell agreed wholeheartedly with Howells, that the incident was out of place in the book. The three readers were not acting as censors, however, because they were happy enough when Twain later published the episode alone in an issue of the Hartford *Bazaar*. They did not disapprove of it for itself; they simply felt that it did not belong in *The Prince and the Pauper.*

That Twain did not always accept the advice which he had requested is illustrated by Parker at the end of his article when he tells of one episode which he and Twichell both agreed should not be included. When the book appeared, the episode was still there, and Parker still did not like it:

> . . . Without speaking of other excisions, one particular thing which both Mr. Twichell and I regarded as a distinct blot on one page, held its course against all suggestions. Of course I shall not indicate the page or the blot.[2]

Mark Twain, then while he sought advice from many of his friends, did not let them make revisions of which he did not approve. In Twain's writing Twichell did not object to obscenity; he did, however, object to blasphemy. On manuscripts which Twain was preparing for publication, Twichell made suggestions only (never acting as censor), suggestions which Mark Twain then followed or not, as he desired. Personal materials which Twain wrote for Twichell's private enjoyment Joe accepted in the spirit in which they were offered, carefully preserving those that were really entertaining, even though they might contain what he would consider vulgarities. He did destroy, however, some things which Twain sent to him as personal letters, and which contained blasphemies or other indiscretions which Twichell did not want to survive because of the possibility of later misinterpretations. He knew that Twain was using him as an "equilibrium restorer," and often, in letters of that nature, was making statements more rash or more vehement than he sincerely meant—or would want preserved as significant ideas of his.[3]

The influence of Twichell on Twain, however, was much more important than mere suggestions on manuscript revisions. First of all, Twain seemed to work well in what might be called the "Twichell atmosphere." Secondly, some of his fundamental ideas, which appear only in works written after the development of the friendship between the two men, seem to have been ideas which he absorbed from Twichell. And, finally, with Twichell's companionship, he was also able to maintain a better psychological balance than he was in the later years when they were not living near each other.

The first indication of the kind of influence exerted by the "Twichell atmosphere" may be seen in a letter which Twain wrote to Howells. Then gathering materials for the January number of the *Atlantic*, of which he was editor, Howells had written to Twain requesting something for that issue. Twain was delighted at the request, because it was well known that the January number was the most special issue of the year, one for which Howells collected materials for some time, saving unusually interesting items which he received during the year to make one especially superior issue. To be requested to submit something specifically for that issue was very pleasing to Twain, who was then most desirous of making his place among the top writers.

Inspiration failed to come, however, and Twain was forced to write to Howells telling him that he could not seem to write anything suitable for the January *Atlantic*. Livy, who knew how important this invitation was to her husband, urged him to get to work and tried diligently to keep the household routine from disturbing him. But in spite of the full co-operation and encouragement of his family, Twain was, for reasons unknown even to himself, unable to write anything at all. He seemed to be completely void of ideas and subject matter, and for long, tense hours, he stared at blank pieces of paper day after day.

Several hours after he sent this unfortunate news to Howells, he wrote again. Twichell had come dashing in just after Twain mailed the first letter and had talked him into going for a hike. He had promised not to discuss Twain's present inability to write and, though he had problems of his own, had guaranteed that they would talk only of pleasant things, hoping to refresh themselves by taking their minds off all their problems for a while. When the conversation turned to their younger days, Twain began reminiscing about his many interesting experiences on the Mississippi River, a topic always fascinating to the Yankee-born-

and-bred Twichell. Recognizing that Twain was happy and excited, Twichell let him go on and on as they tramped through the woods.

As soon as the hike was over and Twain was back at home, he rushed to his desk and wrote to Howells:

> I take back the remark that I can't write for the January number, for Twichell and I have had a long walk in the woods, and I got to telling him about old Mississippi days of steamboating glory and grandeur as I saw them (during four years) *from the pilot-house*. He said, "What a virgin subject to hurl into a magazine!" I hadn't thought of that before. Would you like a series of papers to run through three months or six or nine—or about four months, say?[4]

Life on the Mississippi was the eventual outcome of this walk in the woods, because Twain found that Twichell was correct; this was, indeed, excellent material "to hurl into a magazine," and to assemble later in book form. It is, of course, impossible to claim that Twain would never have written the book if it had not been for Twichell's casual remark. In fact, he undoubtedly would have thought of it himself sooner or later—he had thought of other subjects before meeting Twichell, certainly—nevertheless, on this particular occasion Joe was the catalyzing force which set Twain into action at a time when he was not producing.

Twichell felt that this kind of inspiration also worked in reverse, that he, too, was better able to express himself with Twain around than he could when he was alone. After General Grant's death, which both men felt deeply, Twichell wrote from Vermont:

> I suppose I have said to Harmony forty times since I got up here, "How I wish I could see Mark!" My notion is that between us we could get ourselves expressed. I have never known any one who could help me read my own thoughts in such a case as you can and *have* done many a time, dear old fellow.
> I'd give more to sit on a log with you in the woods this afternoon, while we twined a wreath for Launcelot's grave, than to hear any conceivable eulogy of him pronounced by mortal lips.[5]

When the two men were together their minds seemed to supplement each other to their mutual advantage, and both men seemed to be aware of this.

Sometimes, apparently, reading they had done together, or recommended to each other and later discussed, eventually found a place in Twain's creative processes. There is no evidence that this reading was done with that specific purpose in mind. As friends will do, they merely suggested to each other things which they had enjoyed. Since Twichell, in spite of his classical background, was never a serious scholar, he made no attempt to educate Twain in classical readings, but he did recommend any books to him which he thought the other might enjoy.

He wrote, for example, when the *Rubaiyat* first came to the attention of the people in Hartford via one column of quotations in the *Courant:*

> Read (if you haven't) the extracts from Omar Khayyam on the first page of this morning's *Courant.* I think we'll have to get the book. I never yet came across anything that uttered certain thoughts of mine so adequately. . . . Read it, and we'll talk it over. There is something in it very like the passage of Emerson you read me last night, in fact identical with it in thought.[6]

It is highly probable that on reading the entire work, Joe found that he did not agree with its idea as much as he had seemed to on the basis of reading a few well-chosen selections! More important than his agreement or disagreement with the *Rubaiyat* is the fact that on first seeing it, he could not even wait until he and Mark were together to tell him about it; he had to send him a note immediately, so that they could share this new piece of literature.

As late as 1901, Twain told Twichell that one of the casual items which they had read years before had just then given him an idea for something of his own. He wrote:

> How long it takes a seed to sprout sometimes! This seed was planted in your house many years ago when you sent me to bed with a book not heard of by me until then—*Sherlock Holmes.* [The seed referred to grew into Twain's story, "A Double-Barrelled Detective Story."][7]

Twichell's presence, with his quality of being a good listener and his own rich humor and inventiveness, also inspired Twain to periods of creativity, hard for him to match alone. Again, no claim can be made that Twain could not do this without Twichell, because the early books exist to prove otherwise. Twain himself, nevertheless, recognized that, for some reason, Twichell's presence made things seem more interesting for him to write about.

He suspected this when Twichell had returned to Hartford after their hiking trip together in Europe in 1878. In November he wrote to him:

Joe, if I can make a book out of the matter gathered in your company over here, the book is safe; but I don't think I have gathered any matter before or since your visit worth writing up. I do wish you were in Rome to do my sightseeing for me. Rome interests me as much as East Hartford could, and no more.[8]

That this was not just a complimentary statement, Twain himself recognized when he examined his book, *A Tramp Abroad,* after it was published. In spite of what he had said in the letter from Rome, there is an element of surprise in his discovery of the actual effectiveness of Twichell's presence on his creative mood.

Wanting to call Twichell's attention to this, he wrote a rather detailed letter, specifying the number of pages concerning parts of the trip when Twichell was there, and pointing out specific incidents they had shared and tales they had heard or invented. He said:

MY DEAR "HARRIS"—NO, I MEAN MY DEAR JOE,—

Just imagine it for a moment: I was collecting material in Europe during fourteen months for a book, and now that the thing is printed I find that you, who were with me, only a month and a half of the fourteen, are in *actual* presence (not imaginary) in 440 of the 531 pages the book contains! Hang it, if you had stayed at home it would have taken me fourteen *years* to get the material. You have saved me an intolerable whole world of hated labor, and I'll not forget it, my boy.

You'll find reminders of things, all along, that happened to us, and of others that didn't happen; but you'll remember the spots where they were invented. You will see how the imaginary perilous trip up the Riffelberg is preposterously expanded. That horse-student is on page 192. The "Fremersberg" is neighboring. The Black Forest novel is on page 211. I remember when and where we projected that; in the leafy glades with the mountain sublimities dozing in the blue haze beyond the gorge of Allerheiligen. There's the "new member," page 213; the dentist yarn, 223; the true Chamois, 242; at page 248 is a pretty long yarn, spun from a mighty brief text—meeting for a moment, that pretty girl who knew me and whom I had forgotten; at 281 is "Harris," and should have been so entitled, but Bliss has made a mistake and turned you into some other character; 305 brings back the whole Rigi tramp to me at a glance; at 185 and 186 are specimens of my art; and the frontispiece is the combination which I made by pasting one familiar picture over the lower half of an equally familiar one. This fine work being worthy of Titian, I have shed the credit of it upon him. Well, you'll find more reminders of things scattered through here than are printed, or could have been printed, in many books.

All the "Legends of the Neckar," which I invented for that un-storied region, are here; one is in the Appendix. The steel portrait of me is just about perfect.

We had a mighty good time, Joe, and the six weeks I would dearly like to repeat *any* time; but the rest of the fourteen months—*never*.[9]

On this trip, perhaps more than at any other time, the partner-ship aspect of the creation of the literary product was in evidence. Twichell's own speeches and his writing indicate that he was much more impressive and entertaining in speaking than in writing. It is not difficult to imagine the two men, resting after a long tramp, inventing legends because of their mock sadness at finding a beau-tiful area devoid of charming tales. In recounting previous ex-periences of the trip, they could also embellish them by pointing up the humor. This they often did when they rejoined the Clemens family.

It seems probable that most of the invention would have come from Twain, inspired by a good listener who added details and contributed also his own interpretations and additions. Mark Twain might not have sat down all by himself to invent legends for an unstoried region—it would have seemed a rather silly sort of thing to do alone—but it was a delightful way to pass the time with an understanding friend who was enjoying the tales and even helping in their creation. What started as fun may very well then have needed only Twain's actual writing to make it material for the book. When Twichell was not with him during those other months, he had to struggle for something to say. With Twichell there, the creation was spontaneous; he had only then to write it down.

How often Twichell's influence found its way into the book would be impossible to estimate, because most of the long con-versations between the two were never recorded. That his effect on the creation of *A Tramp Abroad* was both significant and beneficial is obvious.

The book was popular. William Dean Howells set the pattern for other reviewers to follow, as they usually did, in an excellent review of it. Even Twichell was impressed with Howells' review. He was somewhat relieved also, because his frequent presence in the book in true and invented episodes had made him feel appre-hensive about its reception.

The topics covered in *A Tramp Abroad* were comprehensive, including matters such as the dueling customs of German students, the German language, legends, comments about Americans in Europe, incidents which Twain considered examples of thought transference from one person to another, etc. All in all, the book was what Twain had wanted to write, in spite of later critical judgments about it. Twichell's presence on the journey had aided him greatly in its creation. The fact that this kind of influence of Twichell on Twain was good seems evident. Here was no suppression of Twain's creative genius by the Connecticut Yankee Puritan Congregationalist parson of a wealthy church. Here, instead, was a decided contribution to the release and fuller expression of the writer's creativity.

One further aspect of this phase of the influence of Twichell on Twain should be added, though it is not so significant as the inspiration Twain apparently felt in Twichell's presence and from his oral collaboration. If it may be assumed that the appreciation and admiration of a close friend are of help to a creator, then the sincerely given praise which Twichell expressed very often in conversation with and in letters to Twain must have pleased and encouraged him. Always desirous of the approval of his friends, Twain received it enthusiastically from Twichell.

This so-called "Twichell atmosphere," which was so important an influence on Twain's writing, seems even to have functioned sometimes when Twichell himself was not entirely a part of the scene. In 1888, Twain brought the manuscript of *A Connecticut Yankee at King Arthur's Court* to Hartford, though the rest of the Clemens family was not at home, and worked on it at Twichell's. He had been finding composition difficult before reaching Hartford. A letter he wrote to Theodore Crane, a friend in Elmira, is revealing.

Friday, October 5, 1888

DEAR THEO,—I am here in Twichell's house at work, with the noise of the children and an army of carpenters to help. Of course they don't help, but neither do they hinder. It's like a boiler factory for racket, and in nailing a wooden ceiling on to the room under me the hammering tickles my feet amazingly sometimes and jars my table a good deal, but I never am conscious of the racket at all, and I move my feet into positions of relief without knowing when I do it. I began here Monday morning, and have done eighty pages since.[10]

This phase of Twichell's influence on Twain was most prominent during the early years of their friendship, when they were
actually together—in other words, it was a "Twichell atmosphere"
which could not be satisfactorily created at a distance from the
man himself, nor could it be reproduced in letters. Because conversation was so integral a part of it, correspondence was not an
effective substitute, a situation aggravated by the fact that Twichell's writing so often lacked the spontaneity and charm of his
talk. His pen could rarely reproduce his enthusiasm. His writing,
instead, was overshadowed by a touch of formality, perhaps established early in his undergraduate and divinity studies, and which
he apparently could not overcome even in informal letters to his
friends. His awkward sentence structure did not help, either.

One might expect to find in Mark Twain's writing, after the
friendship with Twichell had developed, preachers who would
owe some of their personalities to this one minister whom Twain
had come to know best. In many of his books, ministers appeared:
*The Adventures of Huckleberry Finn, The Adventures of Tom
Sawyer, A Connecticut Yankee in King Arthur's Court, Following
the Equator, Innocents Abroad, The Mysterious Stranger, Personal Recollections of Joan of Arc, The Prince and the Pauper,
Roughing It, Tom Sawyer, Detective*, and *What Is Man?* In two
of them, *Following the Equator* and *A Tramp Abroad*, Twichell
does appear under another name; as Mark Twain admitted, "Harris" was merely a pseudonym for Twichell.

In the other books, however, there seems to be little of Twichell's personality in the characters of the ministers created by
the artist. Some of these clergymen are merely stage props, like
the Rev. Leonidas Smiley in "The Jumping Frog of Calaveras
County," written, of course, before he met Twichell; some serve
to advance the plot without having separate significance as preachers. In the books about the Mississippi the preachers are all portrayed without malice, their good and bad characteristics being
pointed out with the same kind of treatment that Twain gave to
the other characters. Condemnation of them, if it appears, is from
the human point of view, not the theological. In his travel books
he often attacked the greed, selfishness, and even evil of missionaries, priests and other clergymen, but he also praised them when
they deserved it. In the historical novels he attacked the autoc-
racy, intolerance and corruption of the clergy in past periods in
other countries.

He realized that ministers are human beings and, therefore, subject to the weaknesses of mankind, and he criticized them no more than he criticized others for their errors. He knew that there were good clergymen and bad ones, and he never damned all clergymen because of the bad ones.

Ministers were, also, he found, excellent subjects for humorous treatment because of the dignity which their profession required of them. The more dignified the man who slips on the banana peel, the funnier to the observer—and Twain was happy to capitalize on this fact. He neither liked nor disliked ministers as a whole. His view of them, as of other men, was directed toward the individual, not the group.

Twichell did not in any way alter Twain's ideas about preachers as human beings. He felt that Twichell was a good minister—"You have a something divine in you that is not in other men." The fact, nevertheless, that Twichell was good was no surprise to Mark Twain because he had always seen ministers as no different in goodness from any other group of humanity gathered together into one profession. Twichell's interest in the ordinary individual coincided with Twain's and was an idea which they had in common by the time they met. It had been the basis for the friendship between Father O'Hagan and Twichell; they had both been very much interested in the individual and his problems as they had observed the soldiers' lives during the Civil War. Twain's views on this subject paralleled theirs in many ways, particularly in respect and love for the individual.

In Twain's writings, therefore, the *mythus* of the preacher, as it becomes illustrated in his books, is almost completely independent of the personality of the one preacher, Twichell, except as he fits the pattern already established in Twain's thought. He, indeed, must have agreed with much of Twain's opinion here expressed, because he, too, objected to anything which suppressed the individual. Thus, in Twain's presentation of the clergy, Twichell fits in one of the categories Twain had previously established—that of the good and sincere preacher—but Twichell was not the determining factor in Twain's ideas about the clergy; he is only an illustration.

Twain's preacher friends seem to have influenced him very little in his interpretations of the problems of organized religion in his own day. He still believed, as he had before knowing them, that the hazards of organized religion could result in errors as often as in good. When he saw what he considered good elements he approved of them—as he did, for example, in the missionary projects of the Asylum Hill Church. Twichell's scrapbooks contain lists in his handwriting of contributions to the missionaries partly supported by his church. Many of these papers are not even labeled as to name or location of the specific missionary. On a great many of these lists appears the entry "S. L. Clemens," followed by different amounts of money, ranging from $5 up to $25, with an occasional $50. While Twain knew that some missionaries had done as much or more damage than good in the areas to which they had been sent, he knew, too, that they could do some good, and he was obviously willing on many occasions to contribute to missionary causes. In addition to these scattered donations, he gave a yearly contribution to Asylum Hill's local missionary project, that of helping to support the Chinese students who had come to America for an education.

In one of his letters home during the hiking trip in Europe, Twichell had said, "A strange Mark he is, full of contradictions." In Twain's attitudes toward organized religion and the clergy, there are as many contradictions as there are in his other ideas and opinions. While writing "To the Person Sitting in Darkness," damning missionary endeavors, he was contributing to these same projects. While criticizing many of the clergy for their various weaknesses and poking fun at them, he was in close contact with ministers whom he respected and whose opinions he valued highly. The conclusion to be reached from this contradictory evidence seems to be similar to the almost inevitable analysis of his ideas about man in general. While damning the human race, he loved individuals. In a parallel fashion, while seeing evils in organized religion and the clergy, he respected what the sincere pastors were trying to accomplish and recognized the sincerity and worth of such men as Burton, Parker, and Twichell. The result is not as contradictory as it might seem at first glance.

While he may not have changed his ideas about the clergy, Twichell did influence Twain's thinking in one very important way. This influence resulted from Twain's regular attendance at Twichell's church, as well as from their personal discussions. It has been pointed out that one of Twichell's ever-recurring topics in his sermons was the subject of Christian manhood, the quality of being a man in spite of outer circumstances, the ability to retain the best aspects of human dignity in all places.

In his scrapbooks he put copies of a great many of his sermons, and in these sermons the *man* is always emphasized. He believed that man was the crowning product of the creative energy and that this energy was still functioning to make man better and better.

The title of one of these sermons is "The Coming Man." In words which must have sounded very familiar to his congregation because he had used variations on this theme so many times before, he said:

> It is the testimony of revelations and of science alike that the crowning product of the creative energy is man, who was the forethought of the whole work preceding his arrival, and when he arrived a goal was reached. Both agree, also, that though created he is still incomplete; still the forethought of the universal world process, his perfection the goal that is now being pushed for. And his perfection is to be wrought out along the lines of his spiritual nature. The idea expressed by Paul in the words of the text is restated, as far as he goes, by John Fiske, when he says that suffering humanity will in time throw off its brute inheritance; its psychical nature will predominate, and whereas the soul has long been an appendage of the body the body will become the vehicle and appendage of the soul. . . . But while in the race the coming man is bound to be superior to the antecedent man, in the case of the individual this may or may not be so. To how many men does the brute inheritance return, while the spiritual nature retreats. . . . The vital thing with us is to be on the side of our hope of a better manhood, the chief of all concerns committed to our care. Its betrayers are sin and unbelief. Religious doubts you will have; but it makes all the difference whether they are the doubts of an aspiring soul or of a flesh loving, self-indulgent soul—of a rising or of a declining manhood.[11]

On still another Sunday, his sermon was entitled, "What Makes Manhood?" He concluded:

> Christ is the real basis of all true manhood, and to aim at the recognition of the high calling in Him, to be deeply persuaded to see and help one another see, that is calling to nothing less and nothing other, than to the fulfillment of the essential conditions of the largest and truest and freest manhood.[12]

In all mankind, he preached, spiritual evolution is now at work to make man better. The individual man must accept the responsibility of becoming a part of this progress toward perfection, and not allow himself to become a throwback to the brute. But, most of all, a man *can* be a man. There is nothing to keep any man from developing his manhood to the fullest. It makes no difference what temptations he is forced to face, nor what unfortunate circumstances beyond his control may combine to crush him—a kind of manhood which can withstand all ills and go forward with confidence is a complete and unquestionable possibility. Emphasizing one aspect or another of this idea, using it as part of a larger topic, as a topic by itself, or as an illustration of another point, Twichell preached sermon after sermon. Although always expressed differently, this one theme occurs more often than any other. A talk in memory of someone who had died, a sermon about the founding fathers, a retelling of a story from the Bible—in all of these, Twichell used his favorite theme, the one that obviously seemed most important to him. It would be almost impossible to find even one sermon in which the idea was not at least suggested.

That Mark Twain heard some of these sermons was inevitable. Because the topic was such a frequent one, even a churchgoer who attended the Asylum Hill Congregational Church much less often than Twain did could hardly have missed it. The frequency of personal discussions between the two men on freedom of the will, determinism, the individual's responsibility for his own actions may well have resulted from statements made by Twichell in the pulpit. That Mark Twain felt that man deserved no credit nor blame for his actions, which were always beyond his control, was a point in which they could not find agreement, but Twain considered Twichell's views very carefully.

Twichell himself applied his interest in individuals to the production of fiction, if we may credit the words Charles Dudley Warner attributes to him in *Backlog Studies*. He saw variety of personalities as an interesting phenomenon and felt that in men lay the foundations of literary production. As an antidote to Twain's lumping mankind together as the "damned human race," Twichell pointed out other possibilities (in man's manliness). In a conversation about plots of fiction and the possible exhaustion of combinations of events which might lead to sterility in creative art, Warner has Twichell (called The Parson in the book) say to the others:

> Plots are no more exhausted than men are. Every man is a
> new creation, and combinations are simply endless. Even if we

did not have new material in the daily change of society, and there were only a fixed number of incidents and characters in life, invention could not be exhausted on them. I amuse myself sometimes with my kaleidoscope, but I can never reproduce a figure. No, no. I cannot say that you may not exhaust everything else: we may get all the secrets of nature into a book by and by, but the novel is immortal, for it deals with men.

Twichell was, thus, again looking at man, this time in his infinite variety and was also suggesting the application of his ideas about man to the creation of fiction. That he was sincere is indicated by Warner's continuing:

> The Parson's vehemence came very near carrying him into a sermon; and as nobody has the privilege of replying to his sermons, so none of the circle made any reply now.
>
> Our Next Door Neighbor [who is Mark Twain] mumbled something about his hair standing on end to hear a minister defending the novel; but it did not interrupt the general silence.[13]

Added to these sermon subjects and friendly conversations about man and manhood is the fact of Twichell's very masculine personality; a great many descriptions of him by contemporaries and later writers emphasize that he was a "man's man." Twain recognized this, and whether or not it surprised him is not a matter of record, but it may well have done so. He had known real men on the frontier, on the Mississippi River, and in the mining camps of Nevada. Until his acquaintance with Hartford people, particularly Twichell, he had not known very well the kind of person from a more cultured and well-educated background who also had the decided strengths of manhood. Twain had pictured real men as being those involved in jobs requiring much physical labor. With this idea in mind, it seemed to Twain that Twichell's background and present occupation would hardly produce an individual with strong manly character. Boyhood in a small Connecticut town; education at the Lewis Academy (the *Sally* Lewis Academy, at that), Yale, Union, Andover (not one, but *two* theological schools), ministry in a large, wealthy, city church— Twain undoubtedly had very definite ideas about the kind of *man* who would fit this biographical sketch, because, before arriving in Hartford, Twain had not experienced a close friendship with this sort of person. There was no doubt, however, about Twichell's strength of character. He also talked frequently about the kind of courage necessary to and developing from Christian ideals.

After the two men had been friends for a few years, with Twain also attending Twichell's church fairly regularly and listening to the many sermons on the subject of manhood, a new idea began to appear in his writing, an idea which in many ways parallels the Christian manhood theme of the Parson. The idea was that, in spite of anything that happens, a man can be a man, and that this is true on any level of society.

Twain had known about ordinary people on the frontier. But now he began seeing men in a different kind of society who were also real men. His circle of friends in the Nook Farm community he liked and respected, and they were not the everyday, working variety of people he had known previously. They were from a different background from the people he had known in the past, and they held different positions in society: represented were the clergy, business, and literature, primarily.

At the same time that Twain became aware of his friends' qualities, they were becoming more appreciative of his. Twichell began to see very quickly the fineness of his character. Matthew Arnold, who had said, "Oh, he doesn't like that sort of thing," to Mrs. Howells, found that he too liked "that sort of thing," when it was Mark Twain. Edwin Pond Parker recognized the lack of impiety in one story Twain told.

And while all these people were getting to know and like him, Twain was beginning to feel very much at home with them. Once he really knew them, he liked them. With their cultural and educational background, current interests and occupations, and dressed in their dignified eastern attire, they, too, were men.

Twain never changed his idea about man's life being deterministically established. This, for him, was the truth: man is a pawn, controlled by forces over which he has no control, and, therefore, bearing no personal responsibility for anything he does, says, or thinks, deserving no praise for the good, nor blame for the bad or weak. But, gradually, a new idea was added to that. Even though man, the pawn, could not change the direction of his life, even though he could not be the master of his fate, he could still be a man—and being a man was a good thing. This ability belonged to all classes of people and actually could be developed by someone lacking it. Not only could frontiersman and husky, courageous, outdoor men have this quality, but anyone could.

The growth of the idea, its peak in Twain's fiction, and its waning can be noted as coincident with his Hartford years and the years thereafter. In his first novel, *The Gilded Age,* written in collaboration with Charles Dudley Warner, there is little of the idea. All of the central characters, those created by both authors in their individual sections of the book, are reasonably spineless, though perhaps sometimes charming, individuals. Colonel Sellers is a dreamer whose optimistic plans of securing great wealth and fame keep him and his friends in perpetual poverty. Although he is lovable, he is weak and is presented as not being responsible for what he does. He is what he is. The Hawkins family, who follow along in Sellers' grandiose schemes, are likewise little people being swept along by circumstances.

Laura, adopted daughter of the Hawkins family, drifts from one love affair to another, being seduced by Colonel Selby; loved and left by Harry Brierly, an engineer who was involved with Sellers in a railroad land speculation deal which failed; admired by Senator Dilworthy, and involved in unscrupulous dealings in Washington, D. C. Finding Selby again, she murders him when he threatens to leave her. Acquitted by a jury after a spectacular trial, she dies suddenly of a heart attack when she fails on a lecture tour. The relative success of the characters of the sub-plot, Philip Sterling and Ruth Bolton, does not result from any particular strength in their characters. They are really just lucky.

At this time the manhood theme was not part of Twain's thinking. Man as a pawn was foremost in his mind, and he stopped there. The reader may be sympathetic with or amused by the characters, but he does not wish that they would behave in any way different from what they do, because Twain makes him see very clearly that these unfortunate people have no choice. Poor little man is, indeed, a pitiable creature, and the best we can do is to enjoy his antics when they are funny.

The first appearance of this manhood idea in Twain's fiction is in *The Prince and the Pauper,* published in 1882, nine years after writing of *The Gilded Age,* during which time Twain had been exposed to Twichell's ideas very often. When Edward Tudor, Prince of Wales, and Tom Canty, pauper, discover their amazing similarity in appearance and exchange clothes, the Prince is mistakenly driven from the court, and Tom becomes Prince, and then King of England.

Both boys adjust to their new lives, the Prince's ability to endure the hardships of his new life being more significant as an illustration of the "manhood" theme than Tom's adjustment to court life. The change for Tom was, after all, an improvement. All he had to do to "adjust" was to become accustomed to more comfort and more pleasure than he had ever known.

As Edward Tudor wanders through the city of London and the surrounding countryside, the hitherto sheltered and much-protected Prince of Wales is very badly treated. In spite of beatings and other hardships, Edwards retains his nobility of bearing and dignity of manner. Surely, he has become a pawn, completely unable to direct the unfortunate course that his life is taking. He can and does, however, behave like a *man*. Instead of becoming a pitiable creature for whom the reader might feel sorry, Edward becomes a noble creature—not in title, because this he does not have at the moment, but, instead, in manhood.

The Prince is not the only character in the novel who has this kind of strength and dignity. Through his eyes, the reader is shown the unfortunate conditions of the poor people, their mistreatment by Church and State—and the scraps of dignity which many of them are able to retain even under persecution.

Late in the novel, Edward sees his new-found friend Sir Miles Hendon beaten for his, Edward's, sake, and in Hendon's bearing under the blows, the Prince recognizes the quality of manhood, of being able to "take it" with dignity which he himself had been illustrating all along.

> Hendon made no outcry under the scourge, but bore the heavy blows with soldierly fortitude. This, together with his redeeming the boy by taking his stripes for him, compelled the respect of even that forlorn and degraded mob that was gathered there; and its gibes and hootings died away, and no sound remained but the sound of the falling blows. The stillness that pervaded the place when Hendon found himself once more in the stocks, was in strong contrast with the insulting clamor which had prevailed there so little a while before. The king came softly to Hendon's side, and whispered in his ear:
> "Kings cannot ennoble thee, thou good, great soul, for One who is higher than kings hath done that for thee; but a king can confirm thy nobility to men." He picked up the scourge from the ground, touched Hendon's bleeding shoulders lightly with it, and whispered, "Edward of England dubs thee earl!"[14]

In *The Prince and the Pauper*, thus, the idea has appeared—strength and nobility are possible even under extremely bad conditions. The young king bore up well under the problems of his

new life and continually struggled for recognition as the real
King Edward, even when it seemed totally impossible that he
would ever be restored to his throne. Miles Hendon, with serious
personal problems of his own, nevertheless protected the boy and
took the scourging to save him from it. Sir Miles and Edward
are the characters most badly treated in the novel, considering
what their real positions should have been. Sir Miles and Edward,
however, are also the strongest characters. They were men
throughout (even though the boy Edward occasionally gave way
to tears), becoming dramatic portrayals of the idea—a man can
be a man.

In *The Adventures of Huckleberry Finn,* again the idea is
implied, but not completely expressed. Like Sir Miles and Edward
Tudor, Huck and Jim accept the buffetings of fate with dignity.
The Mississippi River carries them from one adventure to another with no choice on their part, but they accept their difficulties and continue to try to solve their problems. A raft on a
powerful river! How better could Twain have symbolized man's
helpless position in life and his inability to control his own
destiny?

In the character of the slave Jim may be seen the strengths of
a real manhood—this in spite of the conditions of servitude under
which he has spent his entire life. He has an independence of
spirit which remains constant throughout the novel, even during
one of the most critical episodes when it looks as if he may be
returned to the bondage from which he has worked so hard to
escape.

Loyalty to the boy Huck, even when Huck has played a trick
on him, is part of his strength. Huck attempts to convince him
that an event which really did occur was only a dream. Falling
for the trick, he explains later to Huck, after the boy has clarified
the situation for him, that a real friend should not do anything
to make his friend feel embarrassed. Huck is ashamed of what
he has done because he was just trying to be funny, without
realizing that he was being very thoughtless. Jim forgives him, but
in this episode it is decidedly Jim who is the stronger and wiser
of the two. Jim's character as it appears in this and other episodes
in the novel is a revealing illustration of the manhood that
Twain saw as possible even to a slave.

Huck, of course, also has much of that independence of spirit.
In the most critical scene in the book, Huck must decide whether
or not he will turn Jim in as a runaway slave. First, he makes

up his mind to send a note to Miss Watson, Jim's owner, letting her know where Jim is.

After making this decision, he says:

> I felt good and all washed clean of sin for the first time I had ever felt so in my life, and I knowed I could pray now. But I didn't do it straight off, but laid the paper down and set there thinking—thinking how good it was all this happened so, and how near I come to being lost and going to hell. And went on thinking. And got to thinking about our trip down the river; and I see Jim before me all the time; in the day and in the night-time, sometimes moonlight, sometimes storms, and we a-floating along, talking and singing and laughing. But somehow I couldn't seem to strike no places to harden me against him, but only the other kind. I'd see him standing my watch on top of his'n, 'stead of calling me, so I could go on sleeping; and see him how glad he was when I come back out of the fog; and when I come to him again in the swamp, up there where the feud was; and such-like times; and would always call me honey, and pet me, and do everything he could think of for me, and how good he always was; and at last I struck the time I saved him by telling the men we had smallpox aboard, and he was so grateful, and said I was best friend old Jim ever had in the world, and the *only* one he's got now; and then I happened to look around and see that paper.
>
> It was a close place. I took it up, and held it in my hand. I was a-trembling, because I'd got to decide, forever, betwixt two things, and I knowed it. I studied a minute, sort of holding my breath, and then says to myself:
>
> "All right, then, I'll *go* to hell"— and tore it up.[15]

All the teaching of the society in which he has lived all his life has made Huck fully aware that the decision he has made is bad. There is no doubt whatsoever in his mind but that he will go to Hell because of what he is doing. Thus firmly convinced that his decision is wrong, he, nevertheless, sticks to it. His own nature tells him that he should not betray his friend. This is not an easy decision for him to make and takes much courage and independence on his part, but he goes through with it, being strong enough to carry out his own natural interpretation of right and wrong, regardless of the teachings of others.

Since Twain was being influenced on this manhood idea by Twichell, and Twichell was a disciple of Dr. Horace Bushnell, it is interesting to speculate—what would Bushnell have thought of Huck's decision to go to Hell? Looked at from this point of view, the whole episode seems to be almost an illustration of one thing which Bushnell emphasized—the importance of reliance on the individual conscience as opposed to unthinking acceptance of teachings of others. He would not have believed that Huck's decision would result in his going to Hell, but he most certainly would have applauded Huck's courage and independence of mind. Bushnell—Twichell—Twain (and Huck)—a line of thought is developing. There is no complete parallelism in their philosophies as a whole, and there is sharp disagreement on many major points, but on this one idea there is agreement at least; and, probably, influence more than agreement.

Huck and Jim, then, are both men in terms of the "manhood" theme which is being noted here in Twain's writing. The author does not intrude to tell the reader this fact, nor do the characters state it directly, but it becomes obvious through the actions, thoughts, and words of the two themselves. Simple, and in many ways uneducated, these two, a homeless boy and a runaway slave, even though they are being buffeted by circumstances which they cannot alter, are also capable of being men. They may not be able to change the course of their lives any more than they can change the course of the Mississippi River which is carrying them on, but they can retain much independence of mind, dignity, and strength no matter what happens.

At one point in the novel, Twain does have a speech relating to the subject of manhood, although it does not have anything to do with Huck or Jim. For the first time in Twain's fiction, however, the idea of manhood is directly expressed, though not by one of the main characters.

When Colonel Sherburn had taken all of the insults from a man named Boggs that he could stand, he shot him. That night a mob came to his home to lynch him. Sherburn stepped calmly out onto the roof of his front porch, holding a gun in his hand, and confronted them. He stared at them until they quieted down; then said:

> "The idea of *you* lynching anybody! It's amusing. The idea of you thinking you had pluck enough to lynch a man! Because you're brave enough to tar and feather poor friendless cast-out women that come along here, did that make you think you had grit enough to lay your hands on a *man*? Why, a *man's* safe in the hands of ten thousand of your kind—as long as it's daytime and you're not behind him. . . .
>
> "You didn't want to come. The average man don't like trouble and danger. But if only *half* a man— like Buck Harkness, there—

shouts 'Lynch him! Lynch him!' you're afraid to back down—
afraid you'll be found out to be what you are—afraid and so you
raise a yell, and hang yourselves onto that half-a-man's coat-
tail, and come raging up here, swearing what big things you're
going to do. The pitifulest thing out is a mob; that's what an
army is—a mob; they don't fight with courage that's born in them,
but with courage that's borrowed from their mass, and from their
officers. But a mob without any *man* at the head of it is *beneath*
pitifulness. Now the thing for *you* to do is to droop your tails and
go home and crawl in a hole. If any real lynching's going to be
done it will be done in the dark, Southern fashion; and when
they come they'll bring their masks, and fetch a *man* along. Now
leave—and take your half-a-man with you"—tossing his gun up
across his left arm and cocking it when he says this.[16]

When the colonel finished speaking, the crowd moved back
away from him. Suddenly, the men broke away from the mob
and scattered in all directions. Buck Harkness, who had been the
leader and whom Sherburn had called "half-a-man," ran off as
rapidly as did the others. One *man* had faced the whole mob and
had killed the mob spirit that was leading them on. Whether or
not Sherburn had been justified in shooting Boggs is relatively
unimportant. It is in his scene with the mob that he demonstrates
his courage and strength.

This idea of manhood, which in *The Adventures of Huckleberry Finn* had been illustrated by action and suggested in the
speech of a minor character, was, finally, very directly presented
in *A Connecticut Yankee in King Arthur's Court,* published in
1889, and written, much of it, in Twichell's house.

One of its first direct appearances is in Chapter XVII when
the Yank sees a man tortured to make him confess to killing a
deer. In spite of his physical suffering, the fellow does not confess.
The Yankee assumes, therefore, that he must be innocent and
insists on his release. Finding that the man is really guilty, the
Yank wonders why he suffered so much instead of confessing.
Then he finds that the poor man endured the torture to protect
his meager property for his wife and child. Confession or conviction would result in the confiscation of his possessions; death
without confession would leave his little property intact.

The Yank says:

Oh, heart of gold, now I see it! The bitter law takes the con-
victed man's estate and beggars his widow and his orphans. They
could torture you to death, but without conviction or confession

they could not rob your wife and baby. You stood by them like a man; and *you*—true wife and true woman that you are—you would have brought him release from torture at cost to yourself of slow starvation and death—well, it humbles a body to think what your sex can do when it comes to self-sacrifice. I'll book you both for my colony; you'll like it there; it's a Factory where I'm going to turn groping and grubbing automata into *men*.[17]

This poor man, of course, was an ordinary person; and it is still not surprising to find Twain (through the Yankee, who serves as author's spokesman on important matters throughout the entire novel) giving him the kind of strength to suffer the torture that he did. His emphasis on the word *men* shows that Twain saw this man's primary virtue resting in his manhood—loyalty to wife and child, courage to protect them to some extent even though he could not save his own life.

More significant, however, is the Yank's recognition of the manhood of the king. Although he disapproved violently of monarchy as a form of government, this Connecticut man liked and respected King Arthur very much.

When Hank and the king were traveling incognito through the country, they were captured and made slaves. When all possible purchasers refused to buy King Arthur, the slave trader decided that he was having difficulty in selling him because of his "style." The next step for him was to "reduce a king's style to a slave's style," as Hank put it. Big, healthy, and powerfully built, King Arthur should have brought an excellent price on the slave market. In spite of all his abilities as a salesman, the slave-trader continued to find it impossible to sell the king, however. When prospective buyers saw Arthur's firm, steady glance, upright bearing, and obvious lack of servility in manner, they decided that he would be too hard to handle and refused to buy. The only solution that occurred to the slave-master was to beat this arrogance out of the king, whose identity, of course, he did not know. And so, for a week he beat him regularly.

The Yank says:

. . . Never mind the details—it will save me trouble to let you imagine them. I will only remark that at the end of a week there was plenty of evidence that lash and club and fist had done their work well; the king's body was a sight to see—and to weep over; but his spirit?—why, it wasn't even phased. Even that dull clod of a slave-driver was able to see that there can be such a thing as a slave who will remain a man till he dies; whose bones you can

break, but whose manhood you can't. This man found that from
his first effort down to his latest, he couldn't ever come within
reach of the king, but the king was ready to plunge for him, and
did it. So he gave up at last, and left the king in possession of his
style unimpaired. The fact is, the king was a good deal more than
a king, he was a man; and when a man is a man, you can't knock
it out of him.[18]

Here were two men completely unable to direct the course of
their own lives. Huck and Jim on their raft on the Mississippi
River are paralleled in this novel by Hank and Arthur as slaves,
with their owner deciding everything for them—including where
they shall go and when. Because they cannot escape, they are
powerless. To Twain, man is still a pawn in the hands of forces
which he cannot control. But Twain has, also, at least a partial
answer to the bleakness of this severe determinism. And that
answer, which Twain had heard Twichell say many times, was
found in the concept of manhood. A man can be a man.

A Connecticut Yankee in King Arthur's Court marks the peak
of this idea in Twain's writing, with his most specific statement
of it being the one quoted about King Arthur: " . . . when a
man is a man, you can't knock it out of him."

The idea is still important, however, in Twain's *Personal Recollections of Joan of Arc.* Joan's strength and fortitude were the
elements of her character which most impressed him. Here he
had excellent material for the idea which had become prominent
in his thinking. Joan of Arc was completely unable to change the
circumstances, forces, and events which were leading to her death.
Her life was being determined by forces beyond her control, but
in spite of that, she retained tremendous courage.

When she was fastened to the stake, she still kept her strength
and dignity. Twain described this scene:

> If any thought that now, in that solemn hour when all trans-
> gressors repent and confess, she would revoke her revocation and
> say her great deeds had been evil deeds and Satan and his friends
> their source, they erred. No such thought was in her blameless
> mind. She was not thinking of herself and her troubles, but of
> others, and of woes that might befall them. And so, turning her
> grieving eyes about her, where rose the towers and spires of that
> fair city, she said:
> "Oh, Rouen, Rouen, must I die here, and must you be my
> tomb? Ah, Rouen, Rouen, I have great fear that you will suffer
> for my death."

A whiff of smoke swept upward past her face, and for one moment terror seized her and she cried out, "Water! Give me holy water!" but the next moment her fears were gone, and they came no more to torture her.

She heard the flames crackling below her, and immediately distress for a fellow-creature who was in danger took possession of her. It was the friar Isambard. She had given him her cross and begged him to raise it toward her face and let her eyes rest in hope and consolation upon it till she was entered into the peace of God. She made him go out from the danger of the fire. Then she was satisfied, . . .

Then the pitchy smoke, shot through with red flashes of flame, rolled up in a thick volume and hid her from sight; and from the heart of this darkness her voice rose strong and eloquent in prayer, and when by moments the wind shredded somewhat of the smoke aside, there were veiled glimpses of an upturned face and moving lips. At last a mercifully swift tide of flame burst upward, and none saw that face any more nor that form, and the voice was still.[19]

Perhaps this portrayal of Joan as brave and capable of enduring physical torture is important to note, also, as an indication that the statement, "When a man is a man, you can't knock it out of him," uses the word *man*, regardless of sex. A minor character, the brave wife whose husband was being tortured in *The Prince and the Pauper*, and a major character, Joan, are women who demonstrate this fortitude which has been called manhood, as well as do any of the male characters.

The novel about Joan of Arc concludes:

It was beautiful to hear the Duke d'Alencon praise Joan's splendid capacities as a general, and to hear the Bastard indorse these praises with his eloquent tongue and then go on and tell how sweet and good Joan was, and how full of pluck and fire and impetuosity, and mischief, and mirthfulness, and tenderness, and compassion, and everything that was pure and fine and noble and lovely. He made her live again before me, and wrung my heart.

I have finished my story of Joan of Arc, that wonderful child, that sublime personality, that spirit which in one regard has had no peer and will have none—this: its purity from all alloy of self-seeking, self-interest, personal ambition. In it no trace of these motives can be found, search as you may, and this cannot be said of any other person whose name appears in profane history.

With Joan of Arc love of country was more than a sentiment— it was a passion. She was the Genius of Patriotism—she was

Patriotism embodied, concreted, made flesh, and palpable to the
touch and visible to the eye.

Love, Mercy, Charity, Fortitude, War, Peace, Poetry, Music—
these may be symbolized as any shall prefer: by figures of either
sex and of any age; but a slender girl in her first young bloom,
with the martyr's crown upon her head, and in her hand the
sword that severed her country's bonds—shall not this, and no
other, stand for PATRIOTISM through all the ages until time
shall end.[20]

In Joan, even the self-interest and selfish motivation, which
in other places Twain had said applied to all human beings,
are lacking.

Twichell liked these characters and saw in them this one basic
virtue which was so important to him. Whether or not he recognized his own influence on the idea that had become dominant
in Twain's analysis of good, thinking individuals, he certainly
did agree with, the method in which they were presented, and he
approved.

After the writing of *Personal Recollections of Joan of Arc,* the
idea of manhood and the strength of character possible for the
human being almost completely disappears from Twain's work.
In *What Is Man?* it does not appear, though it seems from the
evidence of the novels themselves that for some time it was a very
important part of Twain's personal philosophy.

It has been pointed out that in Twichell's belief this manhood
ideal was part of a Christian pattern of life, an attribute possible
to men through spiritual powers. In Twain's writing, the theme
of manhood appears primarily as an idea in itself, without the
Christian background which was at the center of Twichell's
philosophy. References by Twain to spiritual powers on this particular subject are rare, but are not completely missing.

When young Prince Edward pointed out that Sir Miles'
strength of manhood came from One above, he seems to indicate
that it had come as a gift from the One above; whereas, Twichell
was preaching that man himself must make the effort—this ideal
becomes possible because of the Christian revelation, but through
man's struggling toward its accomplishment, not as a gift from God.

In the *Personal Recollections of Joan of Arc,* the Christian
background is more prominent than in any other place in Twain's
presentation of the idea, but this was inevitable because of the
actual events in Joan's life with which he was dealing. It is interesting to see that a spiritual side to the situation is evidenced

in Twain's writing in these two books; but it cannot be called central to it, as it most decidedly was with Twichell.

That Mark Twain took this extremely important theme directly from Twichell is obviously impossible to prove. That he must have heard it often from the Parson is likewise obvious, and since he was prone to gaining much from conversation with his friends, it seems likely that, at the least, much of the idea may be held as dependent on Twichell. The importance of the whole "Twichell atmosphere," which seems to have stimulated Twain to literary creation, substantiates the claim that this idea came from Twichell more than from any other source.

Here, then, is another influence of Twichell on Twain which can hardly be considered detrimental to Twain's literary productions, since he wrote most of his best books during his Hartford years. This element may not be so pervasive as the "Twichell atmosphere," but in certain respects it is, perhaps, even more important because it did influence decidedly the basic nature of the characters and the problems they face in Twain's novels, particularly during the middle years of his productivity as an author when the Twichell influence was greatest.

After Mark Twain moved away from Hartford permanently, he and Twichell obviously saw much less of each other than they had during the comparatively happy Hartford years. In spite of regular correspondence and frequent visits back and forth when Twain was living in New York City and then in Redding, Connecticut, they found that friendship at a distance can never be so close as it can be when the friends are able to dash back and forth at will to see each other, to discuss little problems as well as big ones, and little joys as well as big ones.

It is here that the influence that Twichell had on Twain during the middle years of his writing career becomes more evident. The problem becomes that of determining, or even just noticing what happened to Twain's writing when Twichell was no longer around the corner. This is not to say that one factor alone, lack of proximity of Twichell, explains the decline of aesthetic value in Mark Twain's later work; but it does seem to be true that this one element is important in explaining that decline.

Mark Twain's major works are all from the early and middle periods of his writing career. From the early period, before he moved to Hartford, there are *The Celebrated Jumping Frog of Calaveras County*, 1867; and *The Innocents Abroad*, 1869. From what may be called the middle years there are *The Gilded Age* (with Charles Dudley Warner), 1873; *Adventures of Tom Sawyer,* 1876; *A Tramp Abroad,* 1880; *The Prince and the Pauper,* 1882; *Life on the Mississippi,* 1883; *Adventures of Huckleberry Finn,* 1885; *A Connecticut Yankee in King Arthur's Court,* 1889; *Tragedy of Pudd'nhead Wilson,* 1894; *Personal Recollections of Joan of Arc,* 1896. Among those titles are Twain's major writings, the ones that have survived as still worthy of him.

After 1896, however, he did not produce a major piece of literature, one which can be considered anywhere nearly equal in aesthetic achievement with such books as those which he had written earlier, particularly things like *Life on the Mississippi* and *Adventures of Huckleberry Finn.* Although he published fourteen books after 1900, only an occasional short story, such as "The Man That Corrupted Hadleyburg," is of first quality. Several of the titles are hardly ever mentioned in critical studies of Twain's writing, the literary scholars seeming to prefer to ignore the fact that he was writing in the later years. Not many readers, even ardent Twain admirers, seem to be aware of such works as *A Dog's Tale,* 1904, or *A Horse's Tale,* 1907.

Other works are better known, like the philosophical study *What Is Man?,* but usually because they are important to an understanding of Twain the man and author, not because they are first-rate literary productions.

The reasons for this decline in artistic power are difficult to find, and it is necessary to reject answers which explain similar situations in the writings of other men.

Was Twain simply too old? Senility is certainly not the answer, for his mind remained active and alert until his death. His years of dictating to his biographer, A. B. Paine, are sufficient evidence of this. The essay "The Death of Jean," written shortly after his daughter Jean's death in 1909, and not long before his own death, shows much of the earlier ability, minus humor. He was not too old to write. While old age may explain the decline of achievement in the writings of some authors, it is not the explanation of Twain's comparative failures in his last productive years.

Had he written himself out? The exhaustion of his material is not the answer, either, to this question of "Why?" His own creative theory he had called that of "unconscious absorption." He believed that an author wrote best when he dealt with materials which he had absorbed earlier, not even realizing at the time that he was gathering substance for later artistic use. Because first, or immediate, reactions to people, places, and events are apt to be false, or somehow incomplete, he felt that the author should delay composition until his material had really become a part of himself—had been "unconsciously absorbed" into himself and its true significance had become clearly understood. Then, from this storehouse of memories, he could draw out what he wanted to write about.

This was his theory—and in practice it had worked very well for him. His books about the Mississippi area, dealing with material gathered before he even knew he was going to be an author, were, in general, his best (*Adventures of Huckleberry Finn* and *Life on the Mississippi*). Even though he had also been a notebook-carrier consciously looking for things to write about on some occasions (*A Tramp Abroad*), he did not *need* to have more and more experiences in order to have the necessary ingredients for the creation of literature. As an older man, perhaps not wanting to be very physically active, he still had behind him all the years of "absorbing." He was remembering experiences and observations from these years for Paine. Why did he not make use of them himself? All of his rich experiences and his powers of observation were still at his service.

He did write, for example, one short story based on an incident which had occurred during his Hartford years. The incident involved rumors of a prowler around his Farmington Avenue home. The Clemens family was in New York at the time, but Mark went home to investigate. The "prowler" turned out to be an unemployed mechanic who was calling on one of the maids. The girl was in tears, claiming that she was pregnant and the young man would not marry her. Mark Twain secreted Twichell and a witness in one room, then called the young man in. As the two smoked Twain's well-known, long, black cigars and discussed the situation, they were able to reach an agreement—the man would marry the girl "sometime."

The "sometime" became the immediate present when Mark called Twichell and the witness from one room, the girl from another, and had the ceremony performed on the spot. Although he had sympathized with her predicament and had been willing to help, Twain would no longer have the girl in his employ, so he gave each of the couple a hundred dollars and sent them on their way.

A year later he happened to meet the man in Hartford, and asked him how his wife and child were. He discovered that the couple was still childless! The girl had very successfully tricked

Twain and Twichell into helping her to get the man she wanted.

This story has been related in some detail because it shows that here Twain had excellent materials for fictional writing of his best. Humor with an undercurrent of moral indignation should have made a fine combination for his talents. The story has never been published, however, because it was, according to first-hand report, completely objectionable.

A few years before his death in 1910, Twain was invited to speak in Hartford at a women's literary club, and he stayed, as usual, with the Twichells. One evening he read the story to them. After all, he had written *1601, or, Conversation as It Was in the Time of the Tudors* specifically for Joe and knew that he did not object to broad humor. They had read it together more than once and had laughed merrily over it.

This time, however, he had gone too far, and the Twichells were not at all amused. Harmony was most upset that he would read such a story in her home. Joe, likewise *not* amused by the story itself, *was* amused at the expression on his wife's face. Not once did she interrupt the reading, but she drew her lips tighter and tighter, and her eyes also began to reflect her feeling. The intensity and indignation expressed in Harmony's face did amuse Joe, and he laughed. Mark Twain, unfortunately, thought that it was the story which was entertaining his friend.

The next day Mark and Harmony went to the ladies' literary club. She was not a member, because this was not the kind of organization that a minister's wife would customarily be invited to join. Made up of the socially elite of the city, its membership was drawn primarily from the "first families." Because the guest speaker was staying at her home, Harmony had been invited to attend this one meeting.

Mark Twain began by making a few casual remarks, and then he announced that he would like to read them a story which he had written very recently. He told them that he had wondered whether or not this story would be suitable, but since he had read it to Mrs. Twichell and she had approved, he knew that they, too, would not object to it. While Harmony wished that somehow she might quietly disappear from the meeting, and perhaps from the city, he proceeded to read the story. The ladies, of course, reacted as Harmony had done the previous evening, and many of them left "in a huff."[21]

As long as she lived, Harmony Twichell never completely forgave Mark Twain for this blunder. His rough spots she had

understood and overlooked, as had her husband, but the extremity
of this poor taste she could not condone. The Sam Clemens who
had been her neighbor would never have done such a thing. There
was no doubt but that he had changed a great deal. The younger
Twain would, too, have been much more perceptive in realizing
what her reaction really was while he was reading, and would not
have read a story of this kind to the literary group. Although
Harmony's spontaneous anger changed quickly into wonder and
concern, she still felt that what he had done was inexcusable.

Twain's error in judgment, nevertheless, did not affect the
friendship that had grown throughout the years among these
people. Most important, it made Harmony and Joe see very clearly the change that was taking place in Twain's personality. While
they might regret and even be angry at this indiscretion, they
were even more unhappy about what they saw happening to
Twain himself. Their friendship had been too firmly established
to be seriously endangered, but, chiefly, the Twichells wished
that there was something they might do to restore the charm and
gaiety of the man they now saw becoming lonely and embittered—
and more thoughtless about other people than he had been before.

Looking again at the failure of the story—here were materials
suitable to Twain's talents, but he had failed to create a tale that
could even be published.

Along with the mental ability and the materials, Mark Twain
could still express himself well, also. It is not the actual phrase-
ology and structure of the later works which make them of lesser
value. Plots are clear, diction easy and vigorous; yet the works
taken as wholes are dull and heavy with repetition of simple
points, lengthy explanations of easy matters, and indiscretions in
taste and judgment marring the whole literary effect. Thus, even
with the mental ability, the material, and the technique, Mark
Twain could not write as he had once done. What had happened?

The solution appears to rest in the interrelation of the psy-
chology and the philosophy of the man himself and in Twichell's
influence on both. Although Twain's philosophy did not change
radically during his lifetime, it did become intensified. The Calvinism which he had learned in the church in Hannibal, Missouri,
and had then rebelled against so violently, became, nevertheless,
the determinism of his later years. In his thinking, though he
did not admit it, this Calvinism and determinism are fundamen-
tally the same. In each, man is not free to make his own decisions
and carry them through; his life, instead, is determined by ex-

terior forces over which he has no control. It was not too great a
step for Mark Twain to replace the Calvinistic God with other
determining forces. To him, the most important fact was man's
inability to choose. Since his determinism was Calvinism without
God, it was, therefore, a theory of man's being responsible for
behavior which he could not control. On that one major point,
man's responsibility, he differed from Calvinism completely. It
seemed to him illogical that a man should be blamed for doing
what he could not help doing.

His fullest statement of this philosophy comes in *What Is Man?*
In this essay he says that there is no free will, integrity, or virtue
in mankind. The philosophy is that of complete determinism.
The human mind and will have no power whatsoever to determine
the fate of the individual. He says that people are foolish when
they blame themselves for anything they have done, because the
person's first act in life arranges that life so that the scheme can
never be altered, and nothing can be done to break the links that
have been forged.

He compares the mind to a machine which he saw in Sweden.
This device took a block of wood and turned it into marketable
matches in two minutes. That is the kind of machine that the
mind is; it is a clever machine and can work up the materials
which it has, but it cannot create any material at all. In this
philosophy he took no credit for his own creativity and allowed
none to others.

The whole of *What Is Man?* is an elongated discussion of this
idea of man's mind operating as a machine, grinding out ideas
which it has no ability to create. In the form of a conversation,
the essay becomes dull reading and is too long, but those facts in
themselves show that the idea was so much a part of him that he
wanted to repeat it until he was sure that no one could possibly
misunderstand—or disagree, he hoped.

The same idea he put into fictional form in the story *The
Mysterious Stranger*. The stranger is an angel called, curiously
enough, Satan (nephew of the better-known Satan, who was the
only one of a noble family who slipped). In the small village in
Austria where Satan meets three boys with whom he becomes
friendly, there are the familiar evils of witchcraft, superstition and
hypocrisy which have plagued mankind for centuries. In an early
version of the story, later rejected, Twain had the setting in
Hannibal where he had spent his own boyhood, so we see that

he was not talking about a past time or a faraway place, but was really referring to his own time and location.

Satan shows the boys that man is even lower than the animals because his moral sense has led him into evil which the animals do not know exists, but that man should not be blamed for this, because he is helpless to take any independent action, and is completely governed by forces outside his own control.

Twain also felt that man had no sense of innate good or ability for self-sacrifice, but could only act out what was arranged for him, and that he was entirely selfish. Anything that man did was ultimately for his own good, and for no one else's; but he was not to be blamed for this, because even in this respect he had no choice. This was the nature of the creature called man. Apparent choice between generosity and selfishness was not real choice, because man must inevitably make the decision which will be of greatest value to himself. Twain did not recognize any contradictory elements in his theory; man simply had no choice, and what might seem to be apparent choice led only to a predetermined conclusion because of the nature of the human personality, and that personality just did not contain elements of self-sacrifice or generosity.

From the time that he received his early religious education in a strictly Calvinistic church in Hannibal, Mark Twain had been interested in these matters of determinism and moral responsibility. The fact, also, that his mother used church attendance as punishment probably did not help his orthodoxy. When he left home to become a pilot on the river, he began to read more than he had done before. He had time, and the books were available. He soon, apparently, discovered ideas in opposition to those his church had taught, and more in keeping with his own thinking. From that point on, though he was never able to rid himself completely of his Calvinistic training, he attempted to work out his own answers to basic philosophical and religious problems. The character of some of the preachers he had heard on the frontier had also disgusted him, so that more and more it seemed to him that his own ideas were better than those he had been taught. Books provided proofs of opposing theories; individuals differed; he would do his own thinking. He was, no doubt, pleased when he found statements in agreement with his own thought, but he kept that thought comparatively free from literary or personal influence.

In spite of his philosophical belief that man was not responsible for his actions, Mark Twain had, by temperament, a tendency to blame himself for things that happened, whether or not he was really responsible for the situation. In himself, a conflict developed over this disagreement of his intellectual thought and natural reactions. At one time, he took his small son out for an airing after the child had been ill. The boy caught cold and died; Mark Twain blamed himself—and, perhaps, with at least some justification, because he insisted that he had become so interested in his own thoughts that he had failed to notice that the boy was not sufficiently covered. But this sounds like a conclusion arrived at after the fact, and the doctor had recommended that the child be taken outside.

Twain recommended that his brother take a job on a Mississippi River boat, because he himself had enjoyed his life on the river. When the boat exploded and his brother was killed, Twain blamed himself—and here with absolutely no reason to blame himself for a situation over which he had no control. He did feel, however, that he had caused his brother's death.

He also worried about lesser things, taking responsibility that was not his, and being concerned about his own past actions which other people had already very easily forgotten or forgiven, or, perhaps, had never noticed.

As years went on, experiences kept piling up which added to Mark Twain's gloom. Since he could become upset over trivia, like the unimportant, or long since forgiven, or even imaginary injury to Twichell on the European trip, it is easy to see what an emotional extreme a real tragedy could cause in him.

The deaths of those close to him were emotional experiences from which he had a very difficult time recovering. One of the tragedies which disturbed him most was his daughter Susan's death. Again he blamed himself, as he had years before when his brother and his little son had died. He felt guilty about having been in Europe when Susy died, as if, somehow, his presence might have averted the disaster. He knew intellectually that there was nothing he could have done, but he regretted his absence as if it had contributed to her death.

Financial failures and other personal disappointments added to his growing feeling of depression.

As these troubled times came more and more frequently to Mark Twain, he was less able to cope with them emotionally. While his beliefs and his emotional reactions had been much the same during his earlier years, there had been a long time when his outward life had been more satisfactory. His wife was a good influence and seems often to have succeeded in humoring him out of emotional despair. His "damned human race" remark she used as a joke. When his internal feelings were outwardly expressed in streams of vivid profanity, she tried this release of pent-up emotion for herself to show him how it sounded. Because it sounded ridiculously out of place when coming from her, he laughed—and the dark mood passed.

More and more, however, things happened for which Mark Twain felt responsible, and which made him cry out, "Man is not responsible. Don't blame me!" while he was the only one who was blaming himself. Psychologically, then, he adopted the "wish-opposite" to what he felt emotionally, and more and more frequently he said, "Man is not responsible for anything"; but in his personal life he could not convince himself that this was true.

Because his determinism and pessimism had come as much from his emotional responses to life as from his intellect and reading, when the many emotional disturbances became too numerous and overpowering, he felt the necessity to explain his beliefs more explicitly.

In his earlier writings, these ideas had been in the artistic background. Sometimes, indeed, it is difficult, perhaps almost impossible, to know when to take him seriously and to believe him. He was, first of all, a humorist, and often said things simply for the humorous effect, whether or not he meant them seriously. Years of public speaking had made him ever conscious of a living audience. He had spoken to so many different groups of people from the lecture platform as well as socially that he knew what they liked to hear, what amused them, what made them smile, and what made them think. He always wrote, therefore, with an audience in mind. He read much of his material to his wife and to Joe before sending it to the publisher, and perhaps he had those two in mind occasionally as he wrote, the two who best appreciated him.

In his early writing, thus, the philosophical conclusions were subordinate to the story which he was writing for an audience with whose reactions he was familiar. The river in *Adventures of Huckleberry Finn* may be seen to symbolize the determinism in which the author believed, so that like the stream of life, it carried the characters from one experience to the next. Huck and Jim were unable to carry out their decisions; they definitely planned to stop at Cairo, but the river carried them past it during the night. Man cannot make decisions and carry them out; life goes on as circumstances force it to go. The basic philosophy provides a solid background of ideas on which the story itself rests.

In *The Tragedy of Pudd'nhead Wilson* there are many pessimistic and deterministic statements, but they are amusing chapter headings, not integral parts of the development of the action or the plot. "Whoever has lived long enough to find out what life is, knows how deep a debt of gratitude we owe to Adam, the first great benefactor of our race. He brought death into the world." "Why is it that we rejoice at a birth and grieve at a funeral? It is because we are not the person involved." "If you pick up a starving dog and make him prosperous, he will not bite you. This is the principal difference between a dog and a man." "All say, 'How hard it is that we have to die'—a strange complaint to come from the mouths of people who have had to live."

This use of his philosophy for background and for entertainment is true in almost all of the productions of his early and middle periods of writing.

In his last years, however, perhaps from 1896 until his death in 1910, he could no longer keep the philosophy in its place as artistic background for his writings. Particularly after Mrs. Clemens' death in 1904 was this true. His best and most appreciative audience was no longer available to him. Livy was dead; Twichell was living at a distance. The woman who could and did humor and love him, and the man who could and did advise and befriend him were not there to help him through his emotional crises.

Along with this intensification of his emotional reactions to the events of his life, there is an apparent change in his theory of the purpose of his literary art, the change in theory paralleling the change in emotional response. In the early years, when he was still primarily a humorist, he seems to have seen literature as a means of entertainment, which would also contain ideas of value and of educational benefit. *Innocents Abroad, Adventures of Tom Sawyer, Adventures of Huckleberry Finn,* and the other books of that period of his writing career are aimed first of all at entertaining the audience, just as his early lectures were primarily humorous. Lessons and moral values may certainly be present—for example, Huck's struggles with his conscience about whether or not to turn Jim in as a runaway slave, or the criticisms of other countries in *Innocents Abroad*. His major revisions of the latter before it appeared in book form included toning down the violence of the criticism and pointing up the humor. The humor and entertainment are fundamental in the author's thinking and are not sacrificed to preaching. The early novels are supposed to be enjoyable.

Later, Mark Twain apparently rejected this theory and adopted that of literature for purposes of instruction. The story became less important, the humor was played down, and the idea became supreme. The same ingredients are present—story, humor, and idea—but the emphasis has shifted decidedly to the idea. Books like the *Personal Recollections of Joan of Arc* were written in this second period. Still, however, the power of the artist was in at least partial command, and the balance of the several factors is sufficiently effective for the production of good books, though perhaps not so great as *Huck Finn*.

In the third stage of this changing aesthetic theory, Mark Twain swung completely to the side of didacticism. The story became very unimportant, the humor was rare, and the expression of the idea was the complete objective of the author. In *What Is Man?* the entertainer had become the preacher.

This change in literary theory helps to explain the deterioration of the art only when the personality and special abilities of the artist are considered simultaneously with the shifting theory itself. Mark Twain's best talents seem to have lain in the realms of storytelling and humor; even his satire was most effective when it was most humorous. His emotional despair had unfortunately led him to accept a theory which did not allow him to make the best use of his greatest abilities. Because he was emotionally incapable of writing as he had done earlier in his career, he was forced into turning out works of lesser literary quality. Theory, philosophy, practice, and talent no longer blended into the production of a unified and truly artistic work.

Events had psychologically intensified the emotional aspect of the philosophy, which itself had not changed. The artistic element had become almost completely submerged under these pressures. No longer could the philosophy be simply a part of the artist's background of ideas and be used effectively to add substance and depth to the total production. As Mark Twain felt himself forced by the events of his life to cry out, "Don't blame me," he likewise began to preach, apparently trying to convince himself that if man is not responsible for what happens, then he was not responsible. Instead of telling a good story, he allowed the plot and incidents to be lost in the philosophy. *The Mysterious Stranger* has practically no dramatic tension, and the lengthy conversations are not sufficiently interesting to hold the reader's attention. *What Is Man?* is straight philosophy, and Mark Twain was not primarily a philosopher—his best talents were literary. By presenting only his own views in any detail, he even failed to create a conflict of ideas. While he believed sincerely what he wrote, others have believed the same things. There are no really new ideas in philosophy in these books, because he had no contribution to make to philosophical thought.

When, rarely, he did try to write a story during these years without the strong didactic element—like the story of the mechanic and the maid—and many of the published stories—he was unable to bring to bear sufficient critical analysis and judgment to make it a good story.

His interest, apparently, was no longer that of creating a good tale. His major concern was to explain his philosophy. Psychologically, he had no choice—again and again he had to explain these ideas which might once have been only intellectual decisions, but which had become intensified by emotional experience. Didacticism had smothered art, even in this man whose mental equipment was still good, who still had a "stockpile" of available material which could have been utilized in his literary productions, and who still, very decidedly, had the ability to express himself artistically.

Twichell's place, or lack of it, in this later life of Mark Twain is extremely important. During the period of Twain's best writing, Twichell was often able to spur him on and to help him crystallize his own material. In Twain's letter to Howells we have the evidence of the origin of *Life on the Mississippi*. Again we have Mark's own statement to Joe concerning the percentage of the pages in *A Tramp Abroad* on which Harris appears. *The Gilded Age*, too, had been written during the Hartford years. Mrs. Clemens and Mrs. Charles Dudley Warner had expressed their liking for certain sentimental novels of the day which their husbands did not like. Accepting with good nature the disapproval of the men only to a certain point, they had countered with, "Can you do better?" and Twain and Warner had begun work on *The Gilded Age*, the first major fictional work for both of them. During the writing, Twichell had been right there, reading the sections as the authors finished them, and encouraging them in the project. It was not, in this instance, intellectual influence on this work and on many others which Twichell had discussed with their author as they developed so much as it was inspiration, but this was important.

To a man like Twain, whose natural tendency was to withdraw into himself, to brood over all kinds of problems, large and small, Twichell's kind of friendly companionship had been very important. With day by day activities with a man of Joe's personality and enthusiasm for living, a man who was also a close friend, Mark Twain was psychologically better able to maintain the kind of emotional balance that was essential to his writing. How long could he be in a depressed state of mind with Twichell right there waiting to do something, to go somewhere, to talk about something?

The anecdote has been told many times of Twichell's arrival at Twain's on one particular day to talk him into taking a hike with him. Twain was in one of his dark moods of depression and did not want to go. Twichell asked if he would go if he, Twichell, could prove to him that it had been so ordered in the Bible. Taking the challenge, Twain granted that if Joe could prove that the Bible said he must go, then he would. Whereupon Twichell quoted to him, "If a man ask you to go one mile with him, go with him *twain*."

Brought out of his feeling of depression by this trickery, Twain joined Twichell, and they took one of their many enjoyable hikes together, walking, talking, laughing, joking—the usual pattern for this frequent activity. It may never have happened, but, more important, it could have happened. It sounds like something which did occur because it fits the personalities of both men so well and underlines the nature of their relationship.

It is undeniable that during these happy years Twain did not experience the psychological intensification of his intellectual theory which made his later works so often unsatisfactory. While experiences and troubles had much to do with the emotional despair that he later reached, he had experiences during the earlier years, too, which could have become emotional crises, because family problems and business failures occurred during the Hartford years as well as later. The deaths of his brother and his son were early tragedies; the Paige typesetting machine business fiasco was a major financial catastrophe—yet no matter how much he suffered over these things, the deep and lasting emotional despair did not overpower his creative abilities until much later.

Joe's continual attempt to help Twain in letters would indicate that he felt he could be of some help, and that, in person, he had been of some help in the past. His desire to be with Twain during these crises, just to walk and talk with him would give evidence of the value of this kind of activity to Twain when the two families were living in Hartford and the two men could be together often.

This attempt at consolation and encouragement by mail was not very successful, however. The walks and talks might have continued to help as they had done in the past, but circumstances made them impossible. This was a decided loss to Mark Twain as he slipped deeper and deeper into gloom, despair, and bitterness, and as his writing became more and more didactic, losing its artistic power.

A look at Twain's works in his declining years shows the difference when he no longer had Twichell to talk things over with, vehemently, but in good spirit, sometimes even humorously—always, however, sanely, with the exuberance and emotional stability of the one reacting favorably on the exuberance and frequent emotional instability of the other. No other person among Twain's many friends and acquaintances had the same kind of relationship with him that Twichell had, nor the same effect upon him and his writing.

The fact that Twichell was no longer able to accomplish as much when geographical distance made it impossible for them to be together frequently is hardly the fault of either man. Circumstances kept Twichell busy with many, heavy parish responsibilities in Hartford; he was also involved in other activities, important and time-consuming—and could not neglect these things. Circumstances forced Mark Twain into establishing residence abroad, then in New York City, and, finally, in Redding, Connecticut.

Although it would be impossible to blame the comparative failure of Mark Twain's later work completely on the one fact that he was no longer near Twichell, who had helped him so greatly in earlier years, that very fact is, undoubtedly, an important element in the situation. Mark Twain had, after all, held the same philosophical beliefs all his life, and in the early and middle period writings had been able to make good use of these ideas in his literary creations. He was in tune with much of the current thought of his time and wrote for a public ready to listen to him. His ever-delightful humor had permeated his work and had made much of his writing extremely enjoyable as well as thought-provoking. Even his inconsistencies had not bothered the public. His belief in his own literary theory of "unconscious absorption" had been vitally useful to him in his writing. That he had absorbed the Mississippi days of his youth was not only obvious in *Adventures of Tom Sawyer, Adventures of Huckleberry Finn, Life on the Mississippi,* and other books, but was also apparent even in *A Connecticut Yankee in King Arthur's Court.* His readers, however, even those in Connecticut, do not seem to have objected to his Yank's ability with a rope, an art not really much practiced by employees of Colt's Firearms in Hartford. When the Yank compared a lovely scene to one in Missouri, this had seemed all right to those reading the novel. Inconsistencies of all kinds in Mark Twain mattered little in the light of the effectiveness of his total production. He was an artist and created with sure skill and great ability during much of his lifetime.

In the later years, however, when he was emotionally and psychologically unable to keep his beliefs in the artistic background of his writing, he began to preach, and his work began to deteriorate. While Twichell was with him, he was able to maintain the necessary balance. Without Twichell, he failed in that respect, and Joe could only watch it happen from a distance.

What, then, is the total effect of Joseph Hopkins Twichell, the man and the minister, on the writings of Mark Twain? First and of great importance, there is the fact that Twain was able to work well in what has been described as the "Twichell atmosphere."

Second, while Twain did not take many actual ideas from Twichell, who was far from being a scholar in spite of his classical background, he did absorb much of Twichell's belief in the dignity of man, in the ability of a man to be a man in spite of outward circumstances. This idea could, and did, blend in well with Twain's determinism as a supplement to it. Man could not control the course of his life, any more than King Arthur could escape from the slave-trader, but a man could be a man. This idea added much strength to Twain's characters as their lives were pushed in the directions into which the fates led them, and as they suffered because of forces over which they had no control.

Finally, and perhaps most important, Twichell seems to have helped Mark Twain to maintain the necessary emotional balance for the production of art during the years when his influence on Twain was the greatest. That this influence did not continue may be regretted, but its value to the author Twain cannot accurately be estimated.

The total contribution of Twichell to Twain's literary career seems to have been beneficial most certainly, and important enough to give Twichell more claim to fame in the history of American literature than his own writings will ever give him. The circumstances which threw the two men together, in Twain's view, circumstances over which neither of them had a direct control, were of benefit to the American literary scene. This is not a minor contribution from a man whose primary work in life was that of being a minister.

X

Conclusion

NONE OF TWICHELL'S own writings is worthy of serious literary consideration, although he wrote copiously during his long pastorate. Most of his works were of temporary interest and limited value.

Almost every Monday the Hartford *Courant,* edited by his good friend and parishioner Charles Dudley Warner, contained Twichell's sermon from the day before. These have never been collected or published together, but are preserved in the newspaper's files and in Twichell's scrapbooks. From these sermons his theology and homiletic techniques may be determined, but they are not by any means literary treatments of the topics being considered.

Frequently he wrote memorials about people in the church or the community who had died and whose family or friends wanted to publish a little memorial pamphlet. In these memorials he gave the factual details of the person's life and commendation for his fine deeds.

His theological articles, as has been shown, were primarily supplementary materials to Horace Bushnell's more significant contributions.

Twichell's two published books were a biography of John Winthrop entitled, *John Winthrop: First Governor of the Massachusetts Colony,* published by Dodd, Mead and Company in 1891; and an edition of the love letters of Winthrop and his wife, more or less supplementary to the biography, and called, *Some Old Puritan Love-Letters—John & Margaret Winthrop, 1618-1638,* published by Dodd, Mead and Company in 1893. These two books are competently, but not inspiringly, written. He respected Winthrop immensely and wrote his biography from a completely favorable point of view.

Detracting from his written materials was his often extremely awkward style. Typical of the kind of awkwardness in which he could become involved is a sentence quoted previously from a speech given at Yale.

> And if I may be pardoned, I must say that if it were possible that face would be averted from the scene, when it shall happen this afternoon—if so be it shall happen—that an ivy from the grave of Robert Lee, a good man, but the historic representative of an infamous cause, shall be planted on this campus to climb the walls of ever loyal Yale.[1]

By studying the sentence carefully, a reader finds that it can be read; it is complete, and it makes sense. The trick is to put a comma after *possible* in the first line and emphasize the next word, *that*. Since one has to do this with a great many of his sentences, the reading becomes tedious. With sentences as difficult to read as the one quoted scattered throughout his writing, the result is often more confusing than impressive. His style and charm were in his personality and oral presentation, not in his written words.

He also wrote articles about his literary friends in their Hartford homes. One might expect that these would be very interesting to the reader and valuable to the student of literature because he knew so many of these people very well and was with them when they were doing many different things. Not limited to any one particular aspect of their lives, he could have given a most revealing picture of the real human beings with whom he was in almost daily contact. But these articles, like so much of his writing, are of little interest or importance, because, as a gentleman and minister, he, apparently, felt that he could not say anything at all very personal about his friends. He was not a literary critic, so what he had to say about their writings is not particularly valuable. Mark Twain, Charles Dudley Warner, Harriet Beecher Stowe—he described the architecture of their homes, told how well they got along with their families and friends, and, in general, what fine people they were in their personal lives, with no more facts than could be found in a dozen other places, even though he was a man who knew them well. He could have said much more without betraying their confidence in him or revealing private matters. The main value of these essays at the present is limited to the total picture of the friendly relations of the Nook Farm colony which they present.

A complete list of his published works appears in the Bibliography. The volume is impressive, the quality not. His intentions were good; he was intelligent, but his control of the written language was never his strongest attribute. He recognized this and struggled with his writing, laboring over each item; but he was never completely successful in the creation of a well-balanced, interesting, artistic, and valuable piece of writing. He was decidedly not a literary artist himself. In the area of literature, his influence on Mark Twain must stand as more important than anything he ever wrote himself.

During his years of ministry at the Asylum Hill Congregational Church, Twichell's relationship with Mark Twain was, of course, only one part of a very busy life. For him, as well as for Twain, it was an important part of his personal life—a very meaningful friendship which provided him and his family with many pleasant hours.

One of the first things he learned in his civilian ministry was a lesson required of all sincere clergymen—the overwhelming and often frustrating importance of time. It did not take him long after he took over his parish responsibilities to discover that a minister's work is never done; he could work around the clock and still find much that had been left undone. All these things he had to balance almost simultaneously: preparing sermons, administering church business affairs, visiting his parishioners (for the once-a-year visit by the minister to every family in his church was still a custom in Congregational and many other Protestant churches), calling on the sick, the aged, or the distressed, participating actively in community affairs, keeping abreast of current affairs, reading and studying, spending time with his family—and yet always giving the appearance, at least, of having time for each individual, family, or other group in the church or the community who wanted him. The kind of careful planning that all these things required was completely new to him, and he was not prepared to handle these matters smoothly.

He made the mistakes during the first few months that, undoubtedly, many other preachers have made. He tried to reserve Saturday for the preparation of Sunday's sermon. And Saturday after Saturday there were interruptions, sometimes really important, sometimes trivial things which might well have been postponed to another day, but always unavoidable because of his responsibility of being available to his parishioners whenever they wanted him, whether or not it worked in well with his own plans. A change of personal schedule was the only answer to this problem, and he pushed the sermon-preparing-day back to a day earlier in the week. Then when interrupted, he could find another time before Sunday to prepare for the morning service.

Another error which he made during those early days was allowing his family to move into the background of his life, never seeming to have any time for them because of the innumerable church responsibilities. This was not a happy situation for him or his wife and obviously had to be corrected.

Gradually, he was able to solve many of these problems, but it took conscious mental effort and planning for him to keep from being discouraged and frustrated by the things left undone. His friendship with Mark Twain did as much as any other single thing to help him to retain an emotional balance. While his influence on Twain has been emphasized, the value of the friendship was not a one-sided affair. When they talked, hiked, traveled, and when the Twichell and Clemens families did things together, Joe was able to relax more completely than at any other time—and then to return to his responsibilities, refreshed and enthusiastic.

Twain also turned Joe into a notebook-carrier, and he jotted down interesting ideas, descriptions of scenes, experiences, anecdotes, until, eventually, he found that the sermon-creating aspect of his professional career was becoming much easier than it had been at first. In his notebooks, he had more material than he could ever use. Lost for a subject, an illustration, an idea, he had only to browse through the pages of miscellaneous jottings to find a wealth of material.

His first responsibility was always the Asylum Hill Church. After his service as chaplain, he spent his entire professional ministry in this one church. He received many calls to other churches, large and small, particularly after he became more and more well known as a guest preacher at many college chapels, in cities all over the east, and in dozens of churches in Connecticut. Even though many of the offers were attractive, including better salary, larger congregations, etc., he was never tempted to leave Asylum Hill. When asked why, he always said that one of his chief reasons for rejecting these offers was that his family liked Hartford and did not want to move. When another church in that vicinity wanted him, however, even though his residence in Hartford could continue, he turned down the offer as he had all others. Asylum Hill was his church, and he stayed.

At times it seemed as if the members of the church had simply come to take him for granted. Since he had been their minister from the founding of the church, the congregation had never had the full-time services of any other preacher. After he had been there for many years, one of the ladies in the congregation was asked, "How do you like Mr. Twichell?"

"Why," she replied, "he's our minister."

That they did not completely take him for granted, but that they did have a genuine feeling of admiration and respect for him was evidenced on May 27, 1888, his fiftieth birthday when his parishioners presented him the deed of his house. They had spent $6,000 to pay off the mortgage and had collected an additional $4,000 for improvements. After making their plans and collecting the money, the committee in charge had found out that Twichell had received a call to another church. Afraid that he would consider their gift a bribe to keep him at Asylum Hill, they assured him that when they were collecting the money, they had not known about the other offer—and that he was not to feel tied down by what they had done. He had had no intentions of accepting another offer, anyway, and the gift was greatly appreciated by him and his family.

On the whole, it seems evident that Twichell's greatest contribution to his church and its members came in the pastoral, rather than the theological aspect of his professional work. Well educated in doctrinal matters, firm in theological understanding and conviction, he was, nevertheless, not primarily a theologian or scholar; his sermons were adequate and sincere, but not outstanding in any way. Rather was he a pastor to his people, ministering to them in many ways besides preaching on Sunday mornings.

He was always particularly successful with the young people. Having nine children of his own, he had much firsthand opportunity to come to understand the attitudes, ideas, problems, moments of rebellion, and the needs of the next generation. Often when he took hiking and camping trips in New Hampshire and New York, he wrote special letters to all the youngsters in the parish relating experiences, describing scenery, applying Christian teachings where applicable, but never indulging in the overmoralizing or sentimentalizing which many of his contemporaries might well have thought necessary—but which he knew the children would not respect. "None of Joe Twichell's boys ever went wrong" was a trite statement made often of the young men in his church, but it was very close to being true.

The problems of the church, no matter how serious, were somehow always solved without leaving scars of ill will. Differences of opinion that might have led very easily into the formation of opposing groups and parties were always settled before the divisions became permanent and unpleasant, with all participants retaining friendly relations with each other and with their pastor. When this happy situation exists in any church, most of the credit must go to the minister.

As late as 1894, however, there was a crisis in the relationship of the church people with their minister and also with other Congregational churches in the city. The incident itself, with its repercussions and eventual solution, indicates better than any other situation during Twichell's long pastorate, his abilities to smooth over troubled waters, apparently without hurting anyone's feelings.

The beginning of the crisis came at the annual meeting of the Asylum Hill Ecclesiastical Society, the governing body of the church, on March 9, 1894, while Twichell was in Bermuda. Twichell's interest in missionary ventures in this country and in the field of foreign service had resulted for many years in the appearance of a series of solicitors for various causes in the pulpit of the Asylum Hill Church. It was obvious to the solicitors that the financial status of many of the members of this church made it good territory for their requests. Twichell's own sincerity had, perhaps, blurred his vision in seeing that there had been too much of this kind of thing. The church people, therefore, took the opportunity presented by his absence to vote that a change should be made. The real objection was that these solicitors were not only in the pulpit on Sundays, sometimes going through what these sedate Yankees called "gymnastics" unsuitable to the dignity of the church, but, even more annoying, many of them were also apt to follow the men to their places of business on Monday mornings and to the people's homes on Monday evenings. At the meeting Mr. Charles E. Gross stirred up the discussion by proposing a vote that no time during the Sunday morning service be given up to any solicitor. He said that South Congregational Church and Center Congregational Church in Hartford had long before taken similar action which had met with the universal approval of their members.

At that point a heated argument began, with several people saying things that they were long to regret. The first unfortunate and ill-considered remark came from Mr. William H. Moore, who did not agree with Mr. Gross, and who responded, "The result of such a course as that is evident to every one who will compare the donations for benevolent purposes made by the South Church and those by our church. It is one of the results of ruling agents out of the pulpits."

After a few comments by others present, Mr. Frank E. Bliss asked if the society had within its power the authority to pass such a vote. Some of the members of the Ecclesiastical Society were not sure how far their authority extended, and over what matters the minister had complete control. Was this matter something within their jurisdiction? Mr. Gross replied, "Certainly. We hire the minister, we warm the church, and we control the services."

The following resolution was, finally, passed with only two or three dissenting votes:

> Resolved, that in the opinion of this society it is not desirable to have any part of the time for the Sunday morning service given up to any solicitor for any purpose, but nothing herein shall debar Mr. Twichell from presenting any subject himself or prevent Mr. Twichell or the committee from opening the church on Sunday evening or at any other time for such a purpose.[2]

After a full report of the society's meeting—conversations as well as resolutions—appeared in the next day's issue of the Hartford *Courant,* the first objection came from the Rev. Dr. Edwin Pond Parker, Twichell's friend and pastor of the South Church, whose benevolent giving had been mentioned at Asylum Hill's meeting. On Sunday, March 11, before beginning his sermon, Dr. Parker mentioned the report in the paper. He said that it would be discourteous for him to comment on the action itself, but since the report had indicated that South and Center Churches had taken similar action, he felt it necessary to point out that South Church's Ecclesiastical Society had never made any such attempt to control the pulpit. When a society interferes to this extent with the pastor in his control of the pulpit, it is time for a change of pastor, according to Parker.

According to the *Courant's* report:

> Going on, Dr. Parker said that the Rev. Mr. Moore's reported comparison of the contributions for benevolent and charitable

purposes by the different churches seemed to him uncalled for, not to say impertinent. The South, in the first place, hasn't in it the means to give that some of the others have, and, in the second place, it has given much toward reducing its own debt. In sixteen years this has been cut down from $40,000 to below $17,000, and benefits the future as well as the present. Still further, Dr. Parker said that the South Church hasn't, and he was thankful it hadn't any statistician going about to figure up for publication every dollar given by anybody connected with it for charity, so that not only our own left hand but every other left hand in the community shall know what little our right hand has done.[3]

Thus the "Church of the Holy Speculators," in a rash moment, had gotten itself into serious disfavor with other Congregationalists in the city, had stimulated controversy among its own members, and had treated its previously "beloved" minister rather badly. And not only had they done all of those things, but the cooperative *Courant,* aware of the news value of events at Asylum Hill, had kept the entire community well informed as to all the details. Twichell's return from Bermuda was looked forward to with a certain amount of apprehension. Parker's comments had indicated that the passing of such a Resolution was a personal insult to Twichell himself and really amounted to an invitation to him to leave Asylum Hill if he could no longer control what was said from his own pulpit.

The Asylum Hill people began to have doubts as to the wisdom of their action when they saw what a storm they had created. Mr. Gross's attempt to smooth matters over with the other churches in the next day's *Courant* merely emphasized the fact that the situation *was* as bad as originally reported, because he dodged the main issues. He made no mention of the unfortunate statement made about South and Center Churches, and he did not attempt to answer Dr. Parker's suggestion that the action was an insult to Mr. Twichell. He did say that there had been two inaccuracies in the paper's report of his remarks. He claimed to have said that the other two churches had an "unwritten law" which kept solicitors out of their pulpits. He also said that he had not made the statement about hiring the minister, warming the church and controlling the services—and then weakened his denial thoroughly by continuing:

. . . But I did and still assume that in our church all parties will cheerfully conform to an expression of opinion, on the part of the society that furnishes the church and hires the minister. . . .

Now, those who were present at our meeting will remember, and those who will read the report as published Saturday morning will observe, that the two reverend gentlemen who opposed my resolution expressed a fear that the resolution might debar Mr. Twichell himself from presenting any missionary cause or prevent the opening of our church on Sunday evenings for that purpose. While satisfied that the resolution did not do this I cheerfully added, however, the concluding sentences of the resolution preventing such a result and the resolution passed.[4]

It was clear that the outspoken Mr. Gross was not going to calm things down. Left to his own undiplomatic ways, he could have created divisions among the divisions, until nobody was speaking to anybody. No apology for the unnecessary criticism of the benevolent giving of the other churches, a reaffirmation of the society's control of the pulpit—if peace were to be re-established, it was time for Mr. Gross to be less vocal.

Expectations of excited controversy when Twichell returned to the city proved to be false, because he absolutely refused to discuss the matter with anyone—which gave even Mr. Gross no audience for his opinions. Twichell granted, without an argument about it, that if the Ecclesiastical Society of the church had passed such a Resolution, then it must be followed. The strength of the Congregational Church's structure rested, he was sure, in the ability of each Society to decide the matters of interest to themselves in a democratic fashion. Decisions thus democratically arrived at could not be put aside arbitrarily by any one person, even the minister.

The strained relationships with the other churches Twichell smoothed over very easily with the assistance of his fellow ministers, especially Parker, who had been most concerned. Parker had been more upset by the implied insult to Twichell in the Resolution than he had been by the uncomplimentary references to his own church. Any minister has members within his church, he knew, who might make unfortunate statements, and for this the whole Society should not be held responsible. When Twichell passed the whole matter over very lightly, Parker was soon pacified—and others forgot. Twichell maintained his usual good relations with his parishioners during the year that followed, making no mention of the controversial Resolution. For all they knew, he had no objection to it. And no solicitors appeared in the pulpit on Sunday mornings.

One year later, on March 9, 1895, the Asylum Hill Ecclesiastical Society had its next annual meeting. Early during the business meeting, Twichell referred calmly to the Resolution of the previous meeting and said that, though he knew that the person who proposed the motion had been actuated by feelings of kindliness, he was surprised, nevertheless, that such a vote should have passed when he had been their minister for twenty-nine years. Even though he treated the matter in his familiar light way, sometimes almost jokingly, it was very obvious to all that he had been disturbed by it. They quickly recognized his tact in ignoring the situation during the year and in waiting for the proper time and place to present his point of view. They became slightly embarrassed by the Resolution that had passed the previous meeting in a moment of excitement. A year's absence of solicitors had, perhaps, also made them feel that the situation had not really been as bad as they had felt a year before.

After Twichell had retired from the meeting, a customary procedure to allow the Society complete freedom in its deliberations, a vote was taken to rescind and expunge from the records the Resolution passed the previous year. Mr. C. J. Burnell made the motion, and the vote was unanimous.[5]

Thus a situation that might have caused a serious break between pastor and parishioners and among the members themselves, a situation that even the calm Parker had felt would lead to trouble, had been handled very diplomatically by Twichell. Understanding and liking people as he did, he could deal with this kind of crisis without feeling himself personally insulted. It was a business matter for the governing body of the church, and he did not allow personalities to enter into it.

While this episode was, perhaps, the most difficult that he had to handle during the forty-seven years of his pastorate, there were many less important ones which he took care of equally well. There were also occasional problems with individuals in the parish. Once in a while, there were warring factions over practical matters like pew rentals and similar problems. There was also, infrequently, one person who was peeved with the pastor.

One of these people was the ardent suffragist, spiritualist, liberal Congregationalist, and eventually Unitarian, Isabella Beecher Hooker. Although she and her husband were actually members of Park Church until after the Rev. Nathaniel J. Burton's death in 1887, their residence in the Nook Farm community made them a part of the activities of the people there, most of whom were members of the Asylum Hill Church.

Mrs. Hooker thoroughly disliked Twichell and nothing he could do, even ignoring her rudenesses toward him personally and trying to act as if all were well, could make her change her mind. Apparently, her quarrel with him had arisen originally over his lack of willingness to accept her ideas on the subject of spiritualism. As she became more and more rabid on the subject, to the point of fanaticism, she felt that Twichell, who did not agree with her, was intentionally injuring her.

The problem never came to any particular conclusion. Mrs. Hooker continued to dislike Twichell intensely; he went on ignoring her antagonism and attempting to be friendly with her and her husband. The people in the church and in her own family seem to have recognized that Isabella took inexplicable, but violent, dislikes to people. It was unfortunate that there could not be complete accord among the members of the Nook Farm community, but the evidence of only one seriously antagonistic person is surprisingly small when the length of time that Twichell was a part of the Asylum Hill and Nook Farm groups is considered, along with the number of people with whom he dealt during that time.

In his careful organization of his time, Twichell continued all his life to handle his church affairs, to enjoy and care for his family, and to enjoy his personal friendships with Warner, Twain, Lounsbury, and others. One thing he did not have time for, and that was to receive personal honors, although many honors were due him. He was always actively involved in educational matters. He worked diligently with and for the Chinese students who were studying in Hartford and at Yale. He was for many years a member of the Yale Corporation. He also served as a trustee of Atlanta University, in Atlanta, Georgia. In 1865, immediately after the end of the Civil War, the American Missionary Association purchased a railroad box car in Atlanta and began an educational institution for Negroes. The first college class was graduated in 1876. Twichell's contributions as trustee were many, including his interesting some of his moneyed parishioners into contributing to the struggling university.

Because of his contributions to education, and for other reasons (perhaps one unspoken one being his friendship with Mark Twain), several colleges wished to confer honorary doctorates on

him. Spending time to travel to these institutions just to receive
a personal honor seemed completely unnecessary to him.

To each such institution, after receiving their invitation, he
wrote a polite letter, thanking them for considering him worthy
of the honor, but turning them down without explanation. When
Williams College tried to insist, he refused to be pressured and
wrote again, a little more sharply than the first time, saying that
his reasons for not accepting an honorary degree were good and
were known only to himself, which was sufficient. His main reason, which he would not tell the colleges, was that the limited
time which he had for himself was not going to be used for collecting honors, but for recreation and pleasure with his family
and friends.

In his scrapbooks he placed many clippings in which he was
referred to as "Dr." Twichell. Each time, throughout all volumes,
he carefully circled the "Dr." and drew a line into the margin,
where he wrote "Mr."

Finally, after he had retired from his church and had also retired from the Yale Corporation, he accepted an honorary degree
of Doctor of Divinity from Yale University in June, 1913. He had
resigned from the Board of Trustees at their January meeting,
after serving for thirty-nine years. They had voted immediately
to grant the degree, and he had not turned them down. Retired,
he had time to accept this honor, without sacrificing anything
else. No longer did he correct the newspaper articles that called
him "Dr."

One year was particularly tragic for Twichell, who had previously lost very few close friends or members of his immediate
family by death. He had conducted many funeral services during
his pastorate and had tried to comfort the bereaved. In his own
family and among his closest friends, however, there had been
few deaths. All nine children had gone through the various childhood diseases and disasters, but had survived. Young Joe had been
injured in a football game at Yale; Twain had wired from New
York to find out how serious the injuries were. The young man
had recovered quickly, however, as had all the other members
of the family when illness or injury struck.

In 1910, Mark Twain died. For forty-five years the friendship
had stood up under many tests: their separate professional lives,
their different philosophical and theological beliefs, Twain's
"rough spots," Twichell's absent-mindedness—and, in the later
years, not only physical distance, but also Twichell's firm Christian

conviction and Twain's increasing gloom, bitterness, and despair. Forty-five adult years is a long period of time, and it was a no-longer exuberant and enthusiastic man who took the train from Hartford to New York, for Twichell did go immediately to New York to conduct the funeral services for his old friend. He had planned, of course, to go on to Elmira, New York, to conduct the services at the grave, where previously he had conducted services for those so close to Twain, his wife, and his daughters, Susy many years before, and Jean, very recently.

Before the services began in New York City, however, Twichell's sons in Hartford contacted him to tell him that his wife was ill, and he was needed at home. Before traintime he could still lead the service there, but he could not go on afterward to Elmira. His voice broke during his talk at the funeral, and his mind refused to concentrate on one thing. Mark was gone, and Harmony was ill. Twain had said that his relationship with Twichell was "a companionship which to me stands first after Livy's,," and Twichell could have said, and had often thought that his relationship with Twain was "a companionship which to me stands first after Harmony's."

He knew that the 110-mile train trip back to Hartford would be the most difficult journey of his life. He had no idea that Harmony's illness would prove to be fatal; it was enough that she wanted him, and it would take him so long to get there. Although he tried to close his mind to the idea, feeling that it was unnecessary and wrong, he found himself worrying desperately about the possibility of losing Harmony. It would not happen with this illness, he knew, or his sons would have made the message sound more urgent. His mind was still jumping from person to person and place to place: Mark and Harmony; Elmira, and what was happening there, and Hartford, and what he would find there.

As the train entered Connecticut, his seat-companion, who had been stealing glances at him frequently, trying to place him, finally recognized him from pictures, and asked if he were the preacher who had been Mark Twain's friend. Not discouraged by an abrupt and gruff-sounding, "Yes," which did not invite further conversation, the young stranger continued to press him with questions.

"Was Twain as amusing in conversation as he had been in his writing?" "Did he really hate the 'damned human race'?" "How long had they been friends?" "Had Twain ever really gone to his church?"

After a series of brief responses, mostly "Yes" or "No," Twichell startled the stranger by going back to the first question, saying, "Yes, I knew Mark Twain. We first met forty-five years ago in Hartford. . . ."

With little interruption, he talked quietly during the rest of the trip, remembering out loud the whole course of a long friendship and the many things that had happened: Twain's wedding, the pleasures of their young families together, trips to Bermuda, hikes up Talcott Mountain, the European jaunt which Twain had recorded in *A Tramp Abroad*—the gay, the amusing, the serious.[6]

Looking straight ahead most of the time, occasionally glancing at his companion, and occasionally out the window, Joe unconsciously kept track of their progress: Bridgeport, Stratford, New Haven, Wallingford.

Was the stranger a thoughtless lion-hunter, was he really interested, or did he realize that talking would be good for Twichell? Whatever he was, or whatever he was thinking when he posed the questions, he helped Joe emotionally a great deal. Putting all these things into words was good for him, because the words proved again that the forty-five years had been good years. There had been much pleasure that was worth remembering and that submerged much of the pain—and, temporarily, kept his mind from brooding over the trouble at home. He was fortunate on this journey that his seat-companion seemed to be sincerely interested in his reminiscences.

At home, however, he discovered that his sons had not really told him in the telegram how seriously ill Harmony was. Knowing that he would return immediately, they had felt it would be better to tell him very little until he arrived. Harmony seemed to be in a coma when he went in to see her, but, hearing his voice, she roused enough to talk for a while with him, assuring him that she would be well by morning. For a week she had had what the doctors had thought was grippe.

Twichell arrived shortly before seven o'clock on Saturday evening. At eight the doctor decided that the illness was not grippe, but was an intestinal difficulty requiring immediate surgery.

Joe accompanied her at once to Hartford Hospital, where an operation was performed at 11:30 P.M. She died about an hour later. The funeral was held on Tuesday at the Asylum Hill Church and was conducted by the Rev. Dr. Edwin Pond Parker of the South Church, assisted by the Rev. Dr. Francis Goodwin, and the Rev. Dr. William DeLoss Love of the Farmington Avenue Congregational Church, a church which had been built in 1899, directly across Farmington Avenue from Mark Twain's home, on the corner of Woodland Street, where the Twichells lived.[7]

Within a few months, Twichell began to talk about retiring. He was seventy-three years old, and the responsibilities of his large parish had become too much for him. His parishioners were shocked. They had known, obviously, that he would not always be their pastor, but they had not realized that the time had come. Most of the present members had never belonged to any other church. They had never known any other pastor, except guest preachers, or preachers in other churches. The Asylum Hill Congregational Church without Joseph Hopkins Twichell was impossible to imagine. Having had the same minister for forty-five years, the present members of the church had never had the experience of looking for a new minister. They were as much at a loss about what to do as the original founders of the church had been in 1865. Those men who had hired Joe were almost all gone. Their children, grandchildren, and even great-grandchildren were now faced with the same problem of finding a minister for the Asylum Hill Church.

They protested; they assured him that he was still a young man—but he knew better. At the time of Harmony's funeral all of his nine children had been able to be at home except Burton, who lived in California. They had talked to him then about retiring and had urged him to do so as soon as possible. He had reluctantly agreed with their feeling that he was doing more than he should, and nothing had happened to make him change his mind. The desire of the church members to have him remain was pleasing, but impractical.

And so they stalled. After all, they told him, they certainly wanted to take sufficient time to find just the right person to replace him. They joked about it. They pointed out with mock seriousness how tragic it would be if they made a hasty and injudicious choice—only to have the next man stay with them as long as he had!

Realizing that Twichell was serious about wanting to retire, they found, as had the men in 1865, that they really could find a minister, issue a call, and have it accepted. Twichell was, finally, allowed to retire, and on October 1, 1912, the Rev. John Brownlee Voorhees, formerly minister of the Union Reformed Church of New York City, began his duties as minister of the Asylum Hill

Congregational Church in Hartford. Having been educated at Rutgers College and the New Brunswick Theological Seminary and ordained in 1899, Mr. Voorhees had had thirteen years' experience in the ministry. The transition was made more smoothly than any of the Asylum Hill members would have thought possible.

As he had told the people during the two years when he was trying to retire, Twichell did not leave them completely, because he continued to live in the home which they had presented to him twenty-four years previously.

For a few years he continued in some of his earlier activities, taking part in the affairs of the church, seeing friends, lecturing occasionally; but in 1914, his health became so poor that he was rarely able to leave his house. His many friends in Hartford were loyal, visited him, and kept him informed about all the matters in which he had been interested.

Newspapers occasionally sent reporters to interview him, always hoping, probably, that he would say something about Mark Twain or the other famous men whom he had known that had not been said before. One daring reporter from the Hartford *Times*—the friendly *Courant* had never been so indiscreet—even asked him if he had been the one who shot the fireman in New Haven during the town and gown clash between his Crocodile Club and the firemen. He said that he had not fired the shot, but refused to say who had fired it. At seventy-six, he could still keep his reminiscences under control, saying only what he wanted to.

He was ill during his last few years, the nature of the illness not being a matter of record. Perhaps he simply aged rapidly after 1914 and was no longer able to lead an active life. One of his daughters remained with him, the other children visiting frequently. He was very much pleased when his son Joseph Hooker Twichell, named for General Joseph Hooker of the Civil War, under whom Joe had served, enlisted as a chaplain in World War I.

Parish letters sent to Asylum Hill Church's men in the armed forces in World War I said often, simply, "Mr. Twichell is resting comfortably." His daughter wrote the necessary letters to the Veterans Administration regarding his Civil War pension.

He died in 1918, preceded by his wife, his best friend, and most of the original members of his only church, but survived by all nine of his children.

Notes

CHAPTER I

1. Information concerning this episode and the boy's reactions to it are from a speech which Twichell made in 1895, printed in "Record of the Sixth Reunion of the Sally Lewis Academy Association," June 28, 1895, p. 19, in Joseph Hopkins Twichell, ed., *Parish Memorabilia of the Asylum Hill Congregational Church, 1865-1918* (Unpublished scrapbooks, Connecticut State Library, Hartford, Connecticut, 14 volumes) , III:142.

These scrapbooks cover the entire period of Twichell's ministry at the Asylum Hill Congregational Church, plus the six years after his retirement in 1912, until his death in 1918. In them he put anything which was relevant to the church and its members and friends, including Mark Twain, who was not actually a member of the church. Unidentified and unidentifiable newspaper clippings, pages torn from pamphlets and magazines, and letters are mixed with handwritten memoranda of church matters. The scrapbooks, thus, contain a gallimaufry of materials otherwise difficult, if not impossible, to locate. Since Twichell corrected all errors in the printed items by circling the error and writing the correction in the margin, the information is obviously reliable. Volumes and pages are carefully numbered.

Henceforth, throughout this work, this set of scrapbooks will be referred to as *Parish Memorabilia.*

2. Joseph Emerson, ed., *The Evangelical Primer*, pp. 47, 52.

3. George L. Clark, *A History of Connecticut, its People and Institutions*, pp. 354-366.

4. Forrest Morgan, ed., *Connecticut as a Colony and as a State, or One of the Original Thirteen*, III: 274-275.

5. Francis Atwater, ed., *History of Southington, Connecticut*, p. 191.

6. Heman R. Timlow, *Ecclesiastical and Other Sketches of Southington, Connecticut*, pp. 442-443.

7. Julia Merrell, *Talks about a Sheepfold, 1724-1896*, p. 39.

8. Joseph Hopkins Twichell, "Personal Reminiscences," *Bushnell Centenary: Minutes of the General Association of Connecticut at the One Hundred and Ninety-Third Meeting Held in Hartford, June 17, 18, 1902*, p. 70.

9. *Ibid.*

10. Pp. 28-35 from an unidentified pamphlet. Occasion: The Friendly Sons of St. Patrick, 118th Anniversary Dinner of the Society, March 17, 1902, 6:30 P.M., at Delmonico's, New York City, p. 29, in *Parish Memorabilia*, Vl:157.

11. Unidentified clipping, report of sermon by Twichell, in *Parish Memorabilia*, II:6.

12. "Record of the Sixth Reunion . . .," p. 28.

CHAPTER II

1. *Catalogue of the Officers and Students in Yale College, 1855-1856*, p. 34.
2. *Ibid.*, p. 37, and *Catalogue of the Officers and Students in Yale College, 1856-1857*, pp. 29-30.
3. *Catalogue of the Officers and Students in Yale College, 1857-1858*, p. 30.
4. *Catalogue of the Officers and Students in Yale College, 1858-1859*, pp. 30-31.
5. L. H. Baggs, *Four Years at Yale, by a Graduate of '69*, pp. 509-511.
6. *Hartford Times*, April 24, 1914, p. 15.
7. Baggs, p. 511.
8. Timothy Dwight, *Memories of Yale Life and Men, 1845-1899*, pp. 253-254.
9. Robert Stiles, *Four Years under Marse Robert*, pp. 25-36.
10. *Ibid.*, p. 34.

CHAPTER III

1. Carl Sandburg, *Storm over the Land: A Profile of the Civil War*, p. 31.
2. Information concerning Twichell's service, dates, leaves, battles, etc., is from the National Archives of the United States, Washington, D. C., Adjutant General's Office, Old Records Section, where there is a complete folder of his service, containing his enlistment records, statements concerning pay, leaves, absence or presence at Field and Staff Muster-In Rolls, etc.

Information about the 71st New York State is from the National Archives of the United States, Adjutant General's Office, Civil War Section, where there are boxes containing Muster Rolls, Returns, Regimental papers, etc.

3. Joseph H. Twichell, Letter to his father, dated June 9, 1861, quoted in Kenneth R. Andrews, *Nook Farm: Mark Twain's Hartford Circle*, p. 11.
4. *Ibid.*, pp. 11-12.
5. *Ibid.*, April 8, 1862, in Andrews, p. 12.
6. *Woodstock Letters* (Woodstock College: for private circulation, 1878) , VIII: 176.
7. Unidentified clipping in *Parish Memorabilia*, II: 75-76.
8. An unidentified clipping in *Parish Memorabilia*, II: 152, contains the remarks quoted plus the poem. In the margin, in Twichell's handwriting, the initials "J. H. T." have been written. In the Lounsbury papers in the Yale University Library there is a MS copy of the poem with Twichell's signature.
9. Joseph H. Twichell, "Army Memories of Lincoln: A Chaplain's Reminiscences," *Congregationalist and Christian World* (January 30, 1913) , p. 154.
10. *Ibid.*
11. Pages 28-35 from an unidentified pamphlet. Occasion: The Friendly Sons of St. Patrick, 118th Anniversary Dinner of the Society, March 17, 1902, 6:30 P.M. Delmonico's, New York City, in *Parish Memorabilia*, VI: 157.
12. Joseph B. O'Hagan, speech delivered sometime in January, 1872, in Boston, Massachusetts, p. 17.
13. Twichell, "Army Memories of Lincoln," p. 154.
14. Unidentified clipping. Occasion: Laying of the cornerstone of the Excelsior Brigade monument on the Gettysburg Battlefield, July 2, 1888. *In Parish Memorabilia*, II:81-83.
15. See Carl Sandburg, *Abraham Lincoln: The War Years*, I: 495. "Part of it was told in a letter of Chaplain Joseph Twichell of a Connecticut regiment, who wrote his father on July 9 of '62: . . ." Twichell would have crossed out *Connecticut* and written firmly in the margin: "No. 71st N. Y.!"
16. An interesting account of the situation, with another chaplain's views on it may be found in H. Clay Trumbull, *War Memories of an Army Chaplain*, pp. 177-202.
17. *Hartford Times*, April 24, 1919, p. 18.

18. Unidentified clipping, an article signed by Charles H. Owen, in *Parish Memorabilia*, IX: 22.

19. *Hartford Times*, April 24, 1914, p. 17.

20. *Hartford Courant*, n.d., in *Parish Memorabilia*, III: 28.

21. Unidentified clipping. Occasion: Dedication exercises of the memorial to the late President Woolsey, June 22, 1896, address by Twichell. In *Parish Memorabilia*, IV: 8.

CHAPTER IV

1. George L. Clark, *A History of Connecticut, its People and Institutions*, p. 393.

2. *Hartford Courant*, October 15, 1874, p. 2.

3. G. Fox and Co., *A Century in Connecticut*, p. 10.

4. Although no written reference to this has been located, the facts of the little boat's existence and use come from one of Hartford's young "Hucks" who stole it, the late David S. Kennedy (the writer's grandfather) of Hartford, Connecticut.

5. All information concerning the founding of the church may be found in *Manual of Asylum Hill Congregational Church*, a pamphlet published in April, 1867, pp. 3-6. See also Lillian M. Mansfield, ed., *The History of Asylum Hill Congregational Church, Hartford, Connecticut: Centennial 1865-1965*.

6. *Hartford, Connecticut, as a Manufacturing, Business and Commercial Center*, pp. 33-44.

7. Unidentified clipping in *Parish Memorabilia*, I: 5.

8. Incident told by Joseph Hooker Twichell, son of Joseph Hopkins Twichell, July 13, 1950, Washington, Connecticut.

9. Unidentified clipping in *Parish Memorabilia*, X: 68.

10. Charles Dudley Warner, *Backlog Studies*, pp. 167-180.

CHAPTER V

1. Sermon on Dr. Horace Bushnell, preached by Twichell at the Asylum Hill Congregational Church, March 19, 1876, and at the Park Congregational Church, April 2, 1876. Unidentified clipping in *Parish Memorabilia*, I: 79.

2. Quoted in Williston Walker, *A History of the Congregational Churches in the United States*, p. 367.

3. Daniel Dulany Addison, *The Clergy in American Life and Letters*, p. 298.

4. Edwin Pond Parker, *History of the Second Church of Christ in Hartford*, p. 233.

5. Second of two sermons on Bushnell by Twichell. Unidentified clipping in *Parish Memorabilia*, I: 81-82.

6. Joseph Hopkins Twichell, "The Religious Experiences of Childhood," *Hartford Seminary Record*, XVI (August, 1906), 286-292.

7. Nathaniel J. Burton, Edwin Pond Parker, and Joseph Hopkins Twichell, eds., *The Christian Hymnal: A Selection of Psalms and Hymns, with Music, for Use in Public Worship*.

8. Sermon preached by Twichell at the Asylum Hill Congregational Church on the text, "Blessed are the meek for they shall inherit the earth," Matthew 5:5. Unidentified clipping in *Parish Memorabilia*, III: 25.

9. Unidentified clipping in *Parish Memorabilia*, II: 86.

10. Andrew D. White to Joseph H. Twichell, September 4, 1906, in *Parish Memorabilia*, IX: 202.

CHAPTER VI

1. Albert Bigelow Paine, *Mark Twain: A Biography*, I: 370-371.

2. Joseph Hopkins Twichell, "Mark Twain," *Hartford Courant*, April 22, 1910.

3. Quoted by Andrews, *Nook Farm*, p. 250.

CHAPTER VII

1. Albert Bigelow Paine, *Mark Twain, a Biography,* I: 502.
2. *Ibid.,* p. 528.
3. *Ibid.*
4. *Ibid.,* II: 758.
5. *Ibid.,* I: 503.
6. *Ibid.,* p. 621.
7. Mark Twain, *A Tramp Abroad,* Authorized edition, (1921), II: 48.
8. Paine, *Mark Twain, a Biography,* II: 629-630.
9. *Ibid.*
10. *Ibid.,* p. 666.
11. *Ibid.,* p. 630.
12. *Ibid.,* p. 631.
13. *Ibid.,* p. 632.
14. Twain, *A Tramp Abroad,* II: 95.
15. Mary Lawton, *A Lifetime with Mark Twain: The Memories of Katy Leary, for Thirty Years His Faithful and Devoted Servant,* p. 72.
16. Interview with Joseph Hooker Twichell, Washington, Connecticut, July 13, 1950.
17. Albert Bigelow Paine, *Mark Twain's Letters: Arranged with Comment,* II: 508.
18. Joseph H. Twichell, "Yung Wing," *Congregationalist* XXXI (May 21, 1879), 161.
19. Yung Wing, *My Life in China and America,* p. 211.
20. Unidentified clipping, dated October, 1884, in *Parish Memorabilia,* I: 153.
21. Albert G. Mackey, ed., *The Encyclopedia of Free Masonry,* II: 840-841.
22. This investigation was made by Ray V. Denslow, Grand Secretary, Grand Chapter, Royal Arch Masons, State of Missouri, Trenton, Missouri, and stated in a letter to Robert L. Strong, Windsor, Connecticut, March 1, 1950. MS in writer's possession.
23. Joseph H. Twichell, "Mark Twain," *Hartford Courant,* April 22, 1910.

CHAPTER VIII

1. William Dean Howells, *My Mark Twain: Reminiscences and Criticisms,* pp. 32-33.
2. Paine, *Mark Twain, a Biography,* II: 631-632.
3. Unidentified clipping, possibly from the *Springfield Union,* dated December 20, with "'72" in Twichell's handwriting in the margin, in *Parish Memorabilia,* I: 52.
4. *Hartford Courant,* May 13, 1875, p. 2.
See Leah A. Strong, "Mark Twain on Spelling," *American Literature,* XXIII (November, 1951), 357-359.
5. Unidentified clipping in *Parish Memorabilia,* II: 73.
6. Unidentified clipping in *Parish Memorabilia,* II: 74.
7. Unidentified clipping, probably from the *Hartford Courant,* in *Parish Memorabilia,* XII: 186.
8. *Ibid.*
9. Paine, *Mark Twain, a Biography,* II: 591.
10. *Ibid.,* pp. 1156-1158.
11. Paine, *Mark Twain's Letters,* II: 635-636.
12. *Ibid.,* pp. 640-642.
13. Paine, *Mark Twain, a Biography,* III: 1235-1236.
14. Unidentified clipping with the title, "Three of Mark Twain's Old Friends Who Paid Their Tributes to the Great Humorist," in *Parish Memorabilia,* XI: 146.

15. Paine, *Mark Twain, a Biography*, II: 1220.
16. *Ibid.*, p. 1222.
17. Joseph H. Twichell to Mark Twain, August 17, 1904.
18. William Dean Howells to Joseph H. Twichell, October 19, 1910, in *Parish Memorabilia*, XI: 146.

CHAPTER IX

1. Unidentified clipping in *Parish Memorabilia*, II: 74.
2. *Ibid.*
3. Information from Joseph Hooker Twichell, Washington, Connecticut, July 7, 1950.
4. Paine, *Mark Twain a Biography*, I: 531.
5. *Ibid.*, II: 816-817.
6. *Ibid.*, p. 615, footnote.
7. *Ibid.*
8. Paine, *Mark Twain's Letters*, I: 339.
9. Paine, *Mark Twain, a Biography*, II: 666-667.
10. *Ibid.*, p. 874.
11. Unidentified clipping in *Parish Memorabilia*, II: 10.
12. *Ibid.*, III: 115.
13. Warner, *Backlog Studies*, pp. 163-164.
14. Mark Twain, *The Prince and the Pauper*, pp. 227-228.
15. Mark Twain, *Adventures of Huckleberry Finn*, pp. 296-297.
16. *Ibid.*, pp. 204, 205-206.
17. Mark Twain, *A Connecticut Yankee in King Arthur's Court*, p. 147.
18. *Ibid.*, p. 355.
19. Mark Twain, *Personal Recollections of Joan of Arc*, pp. 280-282.
20. *Ibid.*, pp. 287-288.
21. Facts about this incident and story from Joseph Hooker Twichell, Washington, Connecticut, July 13, 1950.

CHAPTER X

1. Unidentified clipping in *Parish Memorabilia*, IV: 8.
2. *Hartford Courant*, March 10, 1894, p. 2.
3. *Ibid.*, March 12, 1894, p. 2.
4. *Ibid.*, March 13, 1894, p. 3.
5. *Ibid.*, March 9, 1895, p. 2.
6. This incident told by Mrs. Dorothy K. Strong (the writer's mother) of Macon, Georgia, who, as a young girl, was sitting in front of the two men on the train and remembers their conversation.
7. Unidentified clipping in *Parish Memorabilia*, XI: 88.

Bibliography

I. Twichell's Published Writing

"The Address by Joseph Hopkins Twichell," *The Monthly Record* (Printed and published by the inmates of the Connecticut State Prison), n. d.

"Appendix: An address by the Rev. Joseph H. Twichell, delivered before the Kent Club of the Yale Law School, April 10, 1878," in Yung Wing, *My Life in China and America.* New York: Henry Holt and Co., 1909.

"Army Memories of Lincoln: A Chaplain's Reminiscences," *Congregationalist and Christian World* (January 30, 1913), 154.

"Baccalaureate Sermon," *The Mount Holyoke,* XII (October, 1902), 51-59.

"Charles Dudley Warner," *Authors at Home,* edited by J. L. and J. B. Gilder. New York: Cassell and Co., Ltd., 1888, 325-332.

"Charles Dudley Warner at Hartford," *The Critic,* VIII (March 14, 1885), n. p.

[With Nathaniel J. Burton and Edwin Pond Parker] *The Christian Hymnal. A Selection of Psalms and Hymns, with Music, for Use in Public Worship.* Hartford: Brown and Gross, 1877.

"The Christian Layman," *Congregationalist,* LXXV (March 20, 1890), 104.

Coleridge Patteson of Melanesia, A Modern Knight. New Haven: privately printed, 1906.

"Concerning Charles Lamb," *Scribner's Monthly,* XL (March, 1876), 720-726.

"Dr. Bushnell in the Woods," *Outlook,* LXV (June 2, 1900), 261-265.

Frank Woodbridge Cheney, 1832-1909. Privately printed pamphlet, no place, n. d.

"George Leon Walker in Hartford," *The Congregationalist,* LXXXV (March 29, 1900), 443-444.

"The Grand Mission of America," *Our National Centennial Jubilee,* Edited by Frederick Saunders. New York: E. B. Treat, 1877, 128-130.

"Harriet Beecher Stowe," *Authors at Home,* Edited by J. L. and J. B. Gilder. New York: Cassell and Co., Ltd., 1888, 315-322.

"A Hartford Admirer's Word of Appreciation," *Congregationalist and Christian World,* (July 10, 1913), 38.

"Hartford, the Birthplace of the Written Constitution," in Willis I. Twichell, ed., *Hartford in History: A Series of Papers by Resident Authors.* Hartford: Plimpton Mfg. Co., 1899, 66-81.

In Memory of Elisha Bliss: A Discourse Delivered by Rev. J. H. Twichell in the Asylum Hill Congregational Church, Hartford, Conn., January 19, 1881. Privately printed pamphlet, no place, n. d.

John Winthrop: First Governor of the Massachusetts Colony. New York: Dodd, Mead and Co., 1891.

Keith-Falconer of Arabia: A Christian Soldier. New Haven: Yale Foreign Missionary Society, 1911.

"Mark Twain," *Harper's New Monthly Magazine,* XCII (May, 1896), 817-827.

Memorial of Samuel Mills Capron. Hartford: Case, Lockwood and Brainard Co., 1874.

Memorial: Rev. Charles Hyde. Hartford: Church Press, 1872, 26-28.

"The Minister as an Angler," *Outlook,* XLI (June 9, 1894), 1018-1020.

A Modern Knight. New Haven: Yale Foreign Missionary Society, 1906.

A Modern Knight of the Cross. Devon, England: Edward J. Manley, Silver Street, Ottery St. Mary, n. d.

A Modern Knight of the Cross: Annual Sermon before the American Board of Commissioners for Foreign Missions. Delivered at Seattle, Washington, September 18, 1905. Boston: American Board of Commissioners for Foreign Missions, 14 Beacon Street, 1905.

"A Modern Saint," Review of *Memorials of the Hon. Ion Keith-Falconer, M. A., Late Lord Almoner's Professor of Arabic in the University of Cambridge, and Missionary to the Mohammedans of Southern Arabia.* By the Rev. Robert Sinker, B. D., Librarian of Trinity College, Cambridge. Cambridge: Deighton, Bell and Son, 1888. *New Englander and Yale Review,* CCXXXI (June, 1889), 381-395.

"More Mark Twain Stories," *London Daily Graphic,* July 18, 1908, n. p.

"Mrs. Harriet Beecher Stowe in Hartford," *The Critic,* XXIII (December 18, 1886).

"Personal Reminiscences," *Bushnell Centenary: Minutes of the General Association of Connecticut at the One Hundred and Ninety-Third Annual Meeting Held in Hartford, June 17, 18, 1902.* Hartford: Case, Lockwood and Brainard Co., 1902, 70-85.

"Qualities of Warner's Humor," *Century Magazine,* LXV (January, 1902, 378-380.

"The Religious Experiences of Childhood," *Hartford Seminary Record,* XVI (August, 1906), 286-292.

"Review" of *The Work of the Holy Spirit,* by Abraham Kuyper, D.D., LL.D., and M.P. Translated by Rev Henri de Vries, and authorized and approved by the author. New York and London: Funk and Wagnalls Co., *Hartford Courant,* October 6, 1900.

Sermon Preached by the Rev. Joseph H. Twichell at the Asylum Avenue [sic] Congregational Church, Sunday Morning, February eleventh, Nineteen Hundred. Hartford: Case, Lockwood and Brainard Co., 1900.

Some Old Puritan Love-Letters—John and Margaret Winthrop, 1618-1638. New York: Dodd, Mead and Co., 1893.

"A Symposium on Expository Preaching, I," *The Old and New Testament Student,* (May 1890), 3-4.

Temptations of the Penitent. Hartford: Printed for the Yoke Fellows Band of the Fourth Congregational Church, Press of the Case, Lockwood and Brainard Co., 1888.

"The United States and China—the Situation," *Advance,* (1879), 102-104.

"The Victorious Bible," *Outlook,* LI (May 25, 1895), 850-852.

"A Word from Another Hartford Disciple," *The Congregationalist and Christian World,* LXXXVII (June 7, 1902), 181-819.

"The Young People's Meeting," *The Congregationalist,* (September 15, 1887), 309.

"Yung Wing," *The Congregationalist,* XXXI (May 21, 1879), 161.

II. Manuscript Sources

Cooke, Rose Terry. *Correspondence of, 1843, 1881-1892.* Connecticut Historical Society, Hartford, Conn.

Healy, Patrick. *Diary, 1878-1879.* 2 vols. Holy Cross College Archives, Worcester, Mass.

Hooker, Isabella Beecher. *Diary, May 11, 1876, to January, 1877.* Connecticut Historical Society, Hartford, Conn.

House Diary, Holy Cross College, 1872-1879. Holy Cross College Archives, Worcester, Mass.

Lounsbury Papers. Yale University Library, New Haven, Conn.

McHenry, J. D. *Letter to Father Murphy, Holy Cross College, September 15, 1911.* Holy Cross College Archives, Worcester, Mass.

Mullaly, John. *Letter to Father O'Hagan,* n. d. Georgetown University Archives, Washington, D. C.

National Archives of the United States, Washington, D. C., Adjutant General's Office, Civil War Section. Information concerning 71st New York State Infantry.

National Archives of the United States, Washington, D. C., Adjutant General's Office, Old Records Section. Folder of Joseph Hopkins Twichell.

National Archives of the United States, Washington, D. C., Veterans' Administration Section, Civil War, Folder of Joseph Hopkins Twichell.

O'Hagan, Joseph B. *Diary, February 1, 1863, to February 19, 1863.* Holy Cross College Archives, Worcester, Mass.

——————. *Speech,* delivered sometime in January, 1872, in Boston, Mass. Georgetown University Archives, Washington, D. C.

Twichell, Joseph H. Letters, Yale University Library, New Haven, Conn.

——————, ed. *Parish Memorabilia of the Asylum Hill Congregational Church, 1865-1918.* 14 scrapbook vols. Connecticut State Library, Hartford, Conn.

Warner Papers, Watkinson Library of Reference, Trinity College Library, Hartford, Conn.

Yale University Faculty Book of Averages, 1850-1865. Yale University Library, New Haven, Conn.

III. BOOKS AND MAGAZINES

Addison, Daniel Dulany. *The Clergy in American Life and Letters.* New York: Macmillan Co., 1900.

Andrews, Kenneth R. *Nook Farm: Mark Twain's Hartford Circle.* Cambridge: Harvard University Press, 1950.

Atwater, Francis, ed. *History of Southington, Conn.* Meriden, Conn.: Journal Press, 1924.

Bacon, Leonard Woolsey. *The Congregationalists.* New York: Baker and Taylor Co., 1904.

Baggs, L. H. *Four Years at Yale, by a Graduate of '69.* New Haven: Charles C. Chatfield and Co., 1871.

Beard, D. "Mark Twain as a Neighbor," *Review of Reviews,* XLI (June, 1910), 705-709.

Bliss, Walter. *Twainiana Notes from the Annotations of Walter Bliss.* Edited by F. M. Edwards. Hartford: Hobby Shop, n. d.

Brooks, Van Wyck. *The Ordeal of Mark Twain.* New York: E. P. Dutton and Co., Inc., 1920 (rev. ed., 1933).

Burton, Nathaniel Judson. *In Pulpit and Parish.* New York: Macmillan Co., 1925.

Bushnell, Horace. *The Age of Homespun.* Hartford: Privately printed, 1851.

——————. *Christ and His Salvation: in Sermons Variously Related Thereto.* New York: Charles Scribner, 1864.

——————. *Christian Nurture.* New York: Charles Scribner, 1861.

——————. *God in Christ.* Hartford: Brown and Parsons, 1849.

——————. *Moral Uses of Dark Things.* New York: Charles Scribner's Sons, 1893.

——————. *Nature and the Supernatural.* New York: Charles Scribner, 1858.

——————————. *The Vicarious Sacrifice, Grounded in Principles of Universal Obligation.* New York: Charles Scribner, 1866.

——————————. *Women's Suffrage: The Reform Against Nature.* New York: Charles Scribner and Co., 1869.

——————————. *Work and Play: or, Literary Varieties.* New York: Charles Scribner and Co., 1871.

"Busy Life of the Rev. Joseph H. Twichell, Mark Twain's Friend," New York *Sun,* February 4, 1912, p. 7.

Catalogue of the Officers and Students in Yale College, 1855-1856. New Haven: Printed by Ezekiel Hayes, 1855.

Catalogue of the Officers and Students in Yale College, 1856-1857. New Haven: Printed by Ezekiel Hayes, 1856.

Catalogue of the Officers and Students in Yale College, 1857-1858. New Haven: Printed by Ezekiel Hayes, 1857.

Catalogue of the Officers and Students in Yale College, 1858-1859. New Haven: Printed by Ezekiel Hayes, 1858.

Cheney, Mary A., ed. *Life and Letters of Horace Bushnell.* New York: Harper and Bros., 1880.

Clark, George L. *A History of Connecticut, its People and Institutions.* New York: G. P. Putnam's Sons, 1914.

Clemens, Clara. *My Father Mark Twain.* New York: Harper and Bros., 1931.

Clemens, Samuel L. *The Complete Works of Mark Twain.* New York: Harper and Bros., Authorized edition, 1921.

——————————. *Mark Twain's Autobiography.* 2 vols. New York: Harper and Bros., 1924.

——————————. *Report from Paradise.* New York: Harper and Bros., 1952.

——————————. *1601, or, Conversation at the Social Fireside as It Was in the Time of the Tudors.* Privately printed by a hell of a printer, 1930.

——————————. *1601, or Conversation as It Was in the Time of the Tudors and Sketches Old and New.* New York: Golden Hind Press, 1933.

Conway, Moncure Daniel. *Autobiography, Memories and Experiences of Moncure Daniel Conway.* 2 vols. Boston: Houghton, Mifflin and Co., 1904.

Davis, Ozora S. *The Pilgrim Faith.* Boston: Pilgrim Press, 1913.

Dexter, Henry M. *Congregationalism: What It Is; Whence It Is; How It Works; Why It Is Better than any Other Form of Church Government; and Its Consequent Demands.* Boston: Nicholas and Noyes, 1865.

Dunning, Albert E. *Congregationalists in America.* New York: J. A. Hill and Co., 1894.

Dwight, Timothy *Memories of Yale Life and Men, 1845-1899.* New York: Dodd, Mead and Co., 1903.

Emerson, Joseph, ed. *The Evangelical Primer.* Boston: Crocker and Brewster, 1844.

Fairbanks, Edward T. *Yale College, Class of 1859, Decennial Record.* New Haven: The College Courant Printers, 1870.

Ferguson, John DeLancey. *Mark Twain: Man and Legend.* New York: Bobbs-Merrill Co., 1943.

Fielder, E. D. "Familiar Haunts of Mark Twain," *Harpers Weekly,* XLIII (December 16, 1899), 10-11.

G. Fox and Co. *A Century in Connecticut.* Hartford: G. Fox and Co., 1948.

Goddard, John Calvin "Joseph H. Twichell—Man and Minister," *The Congregationalist and Christian World,* XC (December 30, 1905), 978.

Grand Lodge Bulletin, Grand Lodge of Iowa, A. F. & A. M., XXXIX (May, 1928), 575-576.

Halsey, Francis Whiting. *Authors of Our Day in Their Homes: Personal Descriptions and Interviews.* New York: James Pott and Co., 1902.

Hartford, Conn., as a Manufacturing, Business and Commercial Center. Hartford: Hartford Board of Trade, 1889.

History of the Class of 1859, Yale College, a Record of Fifty-Nine Years. New Haven: Tuttle, Morehouse and Taylor Co., 1914.

Hornstein, Simon. *Mark Twain: la Faillite d'un Ideal.* Paris: R. Lacoste, 1950.

Howells, Mildred, ed. *Life in Letters of William Dean Howells.* 2 vols. Garden City, New York: Doubleday, Doran and Co., 1928.

Howells, William Dean. *My Mark Twain: Reminiscences and Criticisms.* New York: Harper and Bros., 1910.

Kimball, Arthur Reed. "Hartford's Literary Corner," *Outlook,* LI (June 1, 1895), 903-906.

Larom, W. H. "Mark Twain in the Adirondacks," *Bookman,* LVIII (January, 1924), 536-538.

Lawton, Mary. *A Lifetime with Mark Twain: The Memories of Katy Leary, for Thirty Years His Faithful and Devoted Servant.* New York: Harcourt, Brace and Co., 1925.

Lorch, Fred W. "Mark Twain and the 'Campaign That Failed,'" *American Literature,* XII (1941), 454-470.

Mackenzie, William D. " 'Joe' Twichell and the Boys," *Hartford Seminary Record,* XXII (April, 1912), 131-132.

Mackey, Albert G., ed. *The Encyclopedia of Free Masonry.* 2 vols. New York: Masonic Historical Co., rev. ed., 1929.

Manual of the Asylum Hill Congregational Church. Pamphlet, April, 1867.

Mansfield, Lillian M., ed. *The History of Asylum Hill Congregational Church, Hartford, Connecticut.* Hartford: Asylum Hill Congregational Church, 1965.

"Mark Twain's Pastor: Some Stories of Samuel L. Clemens," *London Daily Graphic,* July 11, 1908.

Masters, Edgar Lee. *Mark Twain: A Portrait.* New York: Charles Scribner's Sons, 1938.

Meagher, Walter J. "Leaves from a Crusader Chaplain's Civil War Diary," *Official H. C. A. A. News,* Holy Cross College publication, Worcester, Mass., n. d, pp. 13, 28.

Merrell, Julia. *Talks about a Sheepfold, 1724-1896.* Hartford: Case, Lockwood and Brainard Co., 1896.

Morgan, Forrest, ed. *Connecticut as a Colony and as a State, or One of the Original Thirteen.* 4 vols. Hartford: Publishing Society of Connecticut, 1904.

Munger, Theodore F. *Horace Bushnell: Preacher and Theologian.* Boston: Houghton, Mifflin and Co., 1899.

"Obituary. Father Joseph B. O'Hagan," *Woodstock Letters,* VIII: 3. Woodstock College, for private circulation, 1878, pp. 178-183.

Obituary Record of Yale Graduates, 1918-1919. Bulletin of Yale University, 15th series, August, 1919, No. 11. New Haven: Yale University, 1919.

O'Hagan, Joseph B. "Chaplains during the Civil War: Two Letters from Fr. Joseph B. O'Hagan," *Woodstock Letters,* XV: 1. Woodstock College, for private circulation, 1886, pp. 111-114.

Paine, Albert Bigelow. "Innocents at Home: How Mark Twain Dictated His Life Story," *Collier's,* LXXV (January 3, 1925), 5-6.

——————————. *Mark Twain, A Biography: The Personal and Literary Life of Samuel Langhorne Clemens.* 3 vols. New York: Harper and Bros., 1912.

——————————. *Mark Twain's Letters, Arranged with Comment.* 2 vols. New York: Harper and Bros., Stormfield ed., 1917.

——————————, ed. *Mark Twain's Notebooks.* New York: Harper and Bros., 1935.

Parker, Edwin Pond. *History of the Second Church of Christ in Hartford.* Hartford: Belknap and Warfield, 1892.

Richards, Alfred T. *History of the Asylum Hill Congregational Church for 1894.* Hartford: Case, Lockwood and Brainard Co., 1895.

Sandburg, Carl. *Abraham Lincoln: The War Years.* 4 vols. New York: Harcourt, Brace and Co., 1939.

——————————. *Storm Over the Land: A Profile of the Civil War.* New York: Harcourt, Brace and Co., 1939.

Schonemann, Friedrich. *Mark Twain als Literarische Personlichkeit.* Jena: Verlag der Frommanschen Buchhandlung, Walter Biedermann, 1925.

Shaw, Bernard. "Meetings with Mark Twain," *Saturday Review of Literature,* XXVII (August 12, 1944), 15.

Shepard, Odell. *Connecticut Past and Present.* New York: Alfred A. Knopf, 1939.

Stiles, Robert. *Four Years under Marse Robert.* New York: Neale Publishing Co., 1903.

Strong, Leah A. "Mark Twain on Spelling," *American Literature,* XXIII (November, 1951), 357-359.

Sweet, William Warren. *Religion on the American Frontier, 1783-1850.* Vol. III: *The Congregationalists.* Chicago: University of Chicago Press, 1939.

Swinton, William. *Campaigns of the Army of the Potomac.* New York: Charles B. Richardson, 1866.

Timlow, Heman R. *Ecclesiastical and Other Sketches of Southington, Connecticut.* Hartford: Case, Lockwood and Brainard Co., 1875.

Tissot, Peter. "A Year with the Army of the Potomac," *United States Catholic Historical Society: Historical Records and Studies,* III: 1 (January, 1903), 42-87.

Trumbull, H. Clay. *War Memories of an Army Chaplain.* New York: Charles Scribner's Sons, 1898.

Trumbull, J. Hammond. *The Memorial History of Hartford County, Connecticut, 1663-1884.* 2 vols. Boston: Edward L. Osgood, 1886.

Twitchell, Willis I., ed. *Hartford in History: A Series of Papers by Resident Authors.* Hartford: Plimpton Manufacturing Co., 1899.

Wagenknecht, Edward. *Mark Twain: The Man and His Work.* New Haven: Yale University Press, 1935.

——————. *Mark Twain: The Man and His Work.* New and rev. ed. Norman: University of Oklahoma Press, 1961.

Walker, George Leon. *Some Aspects of the Religious Life of New England with Special Reference to Congregationalists.* Boston: Silver, Burdett and Co., 1897.

Walker, Williston. *A History of the Congregational Churches in the United States.* New York: The Christian Literature Co., 1894.

Warner, Charles Dudley. *Backlog Studies.* Boston: James R. Osgood and Co., 1872.

——————. *Baddeck, and That Sort of Thing,* in *The Complete Writings of Charles Dudley Warner.* Edited by T. R. Lounsbury, Vol. I. Hartford: American Publishing Co., 1904, pp. 333-465.

Wing, Yung. *My Life in China and America* New York: Henry Holt and Co., 1909.

Index

Joseph Hopkins Twichell

Mark Twain's Friend and Pastor

By Leah A. Strong

Mark Twain described his friendship with Joseph Hopkins Twichell as "a companionship which to me stands first after Livy's." Yet inconsistencies shroud the details of Twichell's life, his friendship with Twain, and his influence over the author.

Twichell was born in Southington, Connecticut, in 1838 and remained there until he entered Yale. After graduation in 1859, he went to New York where he attended Union Seminary. Then, with almost two years of seminary training completed, he enlisted as a chaplain in the Union Army. After serving for three years, Twichell finished his divinity study at Andover and went to Hartford, Connecticut, where he became pastor of the Asylum Hill Congregational Church—the church Mark Twain attended when in Hartford.

Here began a friendship which spanned a period of forty years and terminated only with death. In surveying aspects of that friendship, Dr. Strong analyzes the effect which Joseph Hopkins Twichell had on the man Samuel Clemens, and the writer Mark Twain.